The Untold Story of Frankie Silver

Was She Unjustly Hanged?

Perry Deane Young

Down Home Press, Asheboro, NC

ISBN 1-878086-66-9

Library of Congress Catalog Card Number
98-071449

Book Design by Elizabeth House
Cover Design by Tim Rickard

1 2 3 4 5 6 7 8 9

Down Home Press
P.O. Box 4126
Asheboro, N.C. 27204

Preface

My motivation in writing this book is to set the record straight. It may, thus, surprise the reader to find that the book begins with a re-telling of all the fanciful embellishments that have been added to the bare facts from the time of Charles Silver's murder in 1831 and his wife's hanging in 1833 until now. I did this for several reasons. First of all, it's a helluva tale and never let it be said of me that I let the facts get in the way of a good story. Second, the way stories are passed down, certain facts retained but others completely ignored, is a kind of history all its own. But, the fact remains these are stories and not facts. And, in the writing of history, I insist that the facts are not only stranger than fiction, they often make for a much better story.

Although I was born and reared on a farm near Asheville, both my parents were born in Yancey County and were related to nearly everybody mentioned in the Frankie Silver story. I was told from a very early age that this was a classic story of jealousy and revenge and it was maybe even the original source for the ballad, "Frankie and Johnny." What a shock it was for me to learn at age 22, in 1963, that it was not that at all. To me, the facts present a far more dramatic story than what the balladeers have sung about and I have tried here to present both the untrue stories and the facts, along with all of the original documents relating to the case.

This book is divided into four parts: The first is "the story," with all the embellishments of 165 years of storytellers, balladeers and writers. I don't mean to be overly critical of the authors whose material I have drawn on in this section; in fact, I begin with certain embellishments to the story which I wrote and published myself. The second part involves a search beyond the myths for the facts. The third offers a history of the "confession" or ballad which Frankie never sang from the scaffold. The fourth part presents a transcript of all the original documents relating to the case, along with detailed information on Frankie's family and her descendants through her daughter, Nancy Silver Parker Robinson.

I am grateful to any number of people for their help in preparing this book. Dr. Lloyd Bailey is the dean of historians in this area and his books on the heritage of the Toe River Valley offer a priceless resource for anybody interested in the history of our mountain people. He was there to answer a thousand and one questions for me, as he has been countless times in the past. Lawrence (Larry) Wood was a key figure in helping me to find out what had happened to Frankie's daughter, Nancy. For many years before his death, November 28, 1997, Larry was a major source of information for me on a number of projects. He was always generous with his vast collection of material and never expected any sort of remuneration beyond the joy of sharing it. Dr. Dan Olds of Spartanburg, S.C., provided most of the information on Frankie's (and his wife's) family, the Stewarts. Several of Frankie's descendants provided information on their families and also answered a number of questions about how it was growing up with such a controversial ancestor. I am especially grateful to Peggy Thomas Young, Larry Biddix, Lloyd Hise and Robert Buchanan.

It is my sincere wish that we all see Frances Stuart Silver in a new light, but especially that her descendants recognize that she may not have been a fiendish villain at all, that there may have been another side to the story from what we've been told all these years. She may have been just a poor victim of circumstance. She may have been threatened and simply struck back to save herself, as any of us would do. She may have been unjustly hanged. And it's high time we allowed for that possibility.

Perry Deane Young
Chapel Hill, North Carolina

Contents

Part I: The Legend of Frankie Silver

Tell a Lie When the Truth Would Do 3

Part II: The Search for Facts about Frankie and Charlie

A Personal Confession and Some Important Corrections 17
Chronology...23
The Setting..25
The Silvers 27
The Stewarts...31
Frankie and Charlie...33
"He Treated Her with Personal Violence" 36
She Killed Him in Self Defense...38
Hiding the Evidence...41
The State v. Frankie Silver...44
Morganton Then 45
The Grand Jury Indictment...47
The Members of the Court...49
The Trial and Legal Questions 52
Appeal to the Supreme Court 56
The Efforts to Save Frankie from the Gallows..............................58
The Escape...70
The Confessions 72
The Hanging 78
The Burial 83
Frankie's Child 86
The "Curse" on the Stewarts..92
Morganton Now 96

Part III: Frankie's Song

The Ballad Frankie Never Sang from the Gallows 105

Part IV: Documents

The News of the Day 127
County Court Documents...131
Supreme Court Documents 139
Letters & Petitions 146
More on the Stewart Family 162
More on Frankie's Child...171

Bibliography...191

Part I

The Legend of Frankie Silver

Tell a Lie When the Truth Would Do

There was a time in the mountainbound coves in western North Carolina when bacon fat afrying in the skillet would set the old folks to talking about the way poor Charlie Silver passed on. Wasn't that maybe how he looked and smelled as that spiteful wife of his, the evil Frankie, sat by the fireside all night long, chopping up his body and burning it bit by bit?

Charlie Silver was a strapping young man of 18 when our story begins. He was famous throughout the hills around the Toe River for all kinds of reasons. The girls all thought he was the handsomest catch among the scanty number of young men; and the young men all swore nobody could hoist a long rifle and bring down a buck or a bear as neat as Charlie could. Why, it got so if folks knew Charlie was going to be at a turkey shoot, they'd just not go because they knew nobody could win against Charlie. They claimed he could stand on one ridge and shoot the eye out'n a squirrel on another ridge. And he was the life of the party to men and women alike. Why, it was years and years after he was long gone, dead and burned, when folks would still be talking about the music he could make; near 'bout everybody said he was the best fifer they'd ever heard. If he got carried away every now and again and drank too much, well, he was still young and sowing his wild oats. And what mountain man didn't take a drink?

He was a hard worker and with brute strength and sheer will he wrested a little home place out of a thick forest on an impossibly rugged hillside. He cut the chestnut trees and squared the logs with a broadax and a foot adze, rived the white oak shakes for the roof and stacked the rough field stones tight for a chimney. Soon he had a snug cabin fit for the best looking girl in several counties, Frankie Stewart.

A feisty little blue-eyed blonde, Frankie had come into the mountains with her family. But unlike her new neighbors, she'd been to school. They said she had more "larnin'" than she knew what to do with — and what good was it anyway? Ol' Charlie knew all about staying alive in the wilderness, but when it came to books, he didn't know B from a bull's foot. Frankie said she wasn't going to live with any ignorant man, so during the long, cold winter days she would teach him how to cipher and spell, while he lay on a bearskin rug in front of the fire, his famous white coonskin cap serving as a pillow resting on a little wooden stool.

For a time, they seemed like the happiest couple folks thereabouts had ever seen. With the arrival of little Nancy, their household seemed complete. Charlie carved the baby a little teething ring out of mountain birch and built her a cradle from prized cherrywood. He would dandle the child on his chest when he came in at night and would often rock her to sleep.

And Frankie was every bit as industrious as he was. Among the other women, she had made a name for herself for being able to card and spin three yards of cotton or wool every day, while taking care of the baby and keeping her house spic and span.

But as the months wore on, Frankie devoted more and more time to little Nancy and less and less to Charlie. The baby was now getting all the special attention that had made him so happy before. And he soon drifted back into his old habits. Folks started to whisper about him and old Zeb Cranberry's wife, and word sped back to Frankie about her and all the other women in Charlie's active life away from home.

The Stewarts couldn't help but know Charlie was drinking again. Frankie was too proud to tell them about it, but Charlie was staying out for days and nights at a time and coming home drunk when he came home at all. Frankie didn't have to spell it out for her people, they could see in the haggard lines of her face that she was being abused. One of the neighbors said Charlie thought more of his old hound dog, Drum, than he did of Frankie. All up and down the meanders of the Toe River tongues were wagging. Frankie's daddy let it be known he'd kill Charlie if he ever laid a hand on Frankie or the young'un. The Stewarts had been talking about moving on further West. They'd heard there was free government land up in the new territories northwest of Kentucky. But every time they brought up the subject, Charlie wouldn't hear of it. This was home and he wasn't leaving. And, furthermore, neither was Frankie, not on her life.

It was getting along toward Christmas in 1831 when Frankie knew the weather was right for Charlie to take off on one of his long hunting trips. He never volunteered and Frankie never asked why it took him a week or sometimes two weeks to find the bear meat and venison they needed when the woods closer by were full of game. He arose that morning, December 22, and saw a deep snow had fallen, perfect weather for tracking game.

But Charlie, Frankie said, would you please cut some wood for me before you take off for so long? Charlie cut down a huge hickory tree and sawed and chopped it into just the right lengths to fit their fireplace. Then he stacked it on the porch.

The baby was quiet and Frankie seemed like the pert young girl he'd married as Charlie came in from the cold after a hard day's chopping wood. She had fixed a pot of yams the way she'd learned to cook them back in the low country. She had quail browned to a turn and a pot of precious store-bought rice that had come all the way from Charleston.

Charlie was a happy man as he got up from the table and lay down in front of the fire to play with the baby. "I'll be gettin' out afore daylight, Frankie," he said, as he held the baby up and let it dance on his chest. "So come kiss yer old man goodbye. I won't see ye in the morning. Won't need nothing to eat afore I git to George Young's place, so ye jist stay in bed." She bent over and kissed him one last time.

Frankie would later say there was nobody ever as happy as she and Charlie were when they were sparkin' and even after they were married. She loved him so, she tried to forget when he'd come home drunk and beat her. She feared for the baby, but he never touched little Nancy.

"But I went pert'nigh crazy when it come over me Charlie was goin' with other women," she said.

For months, she schemed and plotted how best to kill Charlie; nobody could cross a Stewart and get away with it. Her daddy told her, "Frankie, if you don't kill him, I will."

"That night, I might'near give up doin' it, but the devil had me, I reckon. Charlie acted like his own self that night. I'd cooked a good supper apurpose fer him. Hit war part of my plan.

"When Charlie went to sleep on the floor after supper, I watched him fer awhile. I got to studyin' about the trouble he'd caused me. But more'n anything, I recollected what Sallie Hildern said to me about Charlie stayin' all night with Zeb Cranberry's wife when he was s'posed to be ahunting. My Charlie lying in that slut's arms!"

Frankie reached down and gently lifted little Nancy from her father's arms and put her to bed. For a long time she watched her sleeping husband, until she finally decided, "If I'm ever going ter to do it, now's the time." Charlie had left the sharpened axe just inside the door and Frankie knew it would be heavy for her.

It was almost as if Charlie had laid his head on the chopping block. He always slept with his head resting on his coonskin cap on a little wooden stool. He had his head turned away from the fire so the light wouldn't keep him awake. Frankie rared back and with all her might lowered the heavy axe onto Charlie's head. But to her horror, that didn't kill him.

Charlie jumped up and screamed, "God bless the child!" And Frankie jumped in bed and hid under the covers with baby Nancy. Finally she heard Charlie fall dead on the floor. She took another lick with the axe and chopped his head clean off, the blood splattering all over the room.

It was late at night and she knew no neighbors or family would be dropping by, but still she had to get rid of the evidence of her horrible deed. There was only one way; she'd have to burn his body in the fireplace. With the axe, she cut him into quarters like she'd seen Charlie section off a deer or bear. Then she took the butcher knife and began chopping up bits and pieces and throwing them into the flames. The fire almost went out until she started stoking it with more and more wood. By morning, she'd gone through that whole tree Charlie had cut up the day before. Still there were parts of Charlie she couldn't get to burn.

She took his head and hid it in an old hollow tree down the hill; some of the bones she threw way back in a little cave she knew about down by the river; other parts she stuffed into an old stone mortar hole the old folks had once used to grind corn. She was too crazy with fear to notice the old dog had taken off into the woods with Charlie's white coonskin cap.

As daylight dawned, she was still scrubbing the flat tops of the puncheon floor with sand and lye until it was almost white. When she finished, she was proud of her handiwork. No sign remained that Charlie's blood had been spilled there.

Frankie took a tree branch and brushed the fresh snow across her tracks around the house. Then she took little Nancy in her arms and went on over the hill to her in-laws to make sure they didn't suspect anything. She bragged, why law, she'd been up since way before sunup doing her wash and scrubbing her floors. And, she said to Charlie's mother, "Ye're hard at it, I see."

"Yes, Frankie, if I work hard now I kin rest these old bones when Christmas gits here."

"Ye haven't seen my man, have ye, Ma?" Frankie asked. "He took Drum and went ahunting up at George Young's place three days back, and I was expecting him back this morning. He knew I had all that meat to get ready for Christmas."

"Don't you worry your brain none about Charlie, chile," said old Mrs. Silver, "he's a pore feller to count on when he gits to hunting."

Old John Silver and his wife both felt their young daughter-in-law was being overly anxious about their Charlie. He was tough; he could take care of himself. He always had. They convinced her to stay with them until he came back. But by the morning of Christmas Eve nobody had yet seen hide nor hair of Charlie. Old man Silver and Frankie set off on the long, cold trip along the river to George Young's house.

A brace of hound dogs met them. Old George himself came to the door when he heard all the barking. "Howdy, folks," Young said, "what fetched you'uns way up here so early in the morning?"

"We're alookin' for Charlie," said John Silver.

"Why, I ain't laid eyes on Charlie since Thanksgiving Day," Young drawled.

"Ye're alyin', George Young," said Frankie. "Ye know where my man is and you're going to tell me."

"Hold your tongue, woman," said John Silver. "There ain't no good reason why George would keep nary nothing from ye about Charlie."

Frankie kept swearing Young ought to know something. Young kept denying. Finally, old John Silver suggested they backtrack to Frankie's and Charlie's cabin and see if they couldn't find any clues to his whereabouts. They were coming over the ridge when a dog started barking at their approach.

"Why it's old Drum," said John Silver. "It's Charlie's dog. I reckon Charlie's come back and all our worrying was for naught." But this was not a happy dog and Silver could sense that something was wrong, dreadfully wrong.

They got to the door of the cabin and it was still securely locked, as Frankie had left it. She pulled out the big iron key and opened the door onto a room that seemed colder than all outdoors. Frankie said Charlie wasn't back 'cause his gun was not where he always hung it, on a peg by the chimney.

Old Drum had followed them into the house and commenced to whine at the feet of Charlie's daddy. "Great God A'mighty," exclaimed John Silver. "Looky there, it's Charlie's hat." There was no doubt about it; nobody else had ever seen an albino raccoon and Charlie had made a cap from the one he killed.

Silver picked up the coonskin. "There's blood on that there cap," he said. "Charlie's dead."

George Young broke the silence: "I don't see why that's a certain cause for worriment. Charlie mought have gunned a b'ar and got blood on that cap of his'n."

Frankie fired back: "Charlie's last words to me were that he was going to your place, George Young. Charlie had his faults but lying wasn't one of them."

John Silver said maybe the dog would lead them to Charlie. "That dog loves my boy and I believe he'll show us where that bloody cap came from." The dog took them down to the edge of the river and stopped by a hole. There was blood splattered around the hole, but nothing they could see inside. Silver frantically dug through the fresh layers of snow, but he found nothing. Old Drum just sat there whining, not understanding what was expected of him.

Convinced his boy had met with foul play but frustrated in his attempts to find him, John Silver made the long trip over the mountains to the county seat at Morganton where he had a long long talk with Sheriff John Boone, nephew of the great Daniel. "Sheriff," Silver said, "my boy Charlie is amissing, and I believe somebody's killed him." The sheriff began using all his inherited hunting skills in the search for Charlie Silver. Near a deep swimming hole formed by a bend in the river, they found Charlie's shoes under a foot of new snow. The sheriff asked for help in breaking the ice and searching with poles through the deep water. They found nothing.

The sheriff listened to Frankie's claim that George Young had to know something, and her brother Jackson wasted no time in telling the sheriff that far from being hunting buddies, there was bad blood between them because Charlie had failed to pay back a loan from Young. Some of the neighbors were saying maybe the sheriff ought to be talking to Zeb Cranberry, who'd come back from a long trip to the markets in Charleston to hear all the talk about his wife and Charlie Silver.

Old man Silver, meanwhile, grew impatient with the sheriff's investigation. He had heard about a black slave owned by Col. Silas Williams over in Tennessee. It was more than a 40-mile walk each way, but Silver went to fetch this "Guinea Negro conjure man," who was famous for finding lost objects and people by using a little glass divining ball.

"I had to pay Colonel Williams ten dollars and scare the black man with a gun to git him over here," Silver said, "but here he is so let's see what he can do."

Word spread quickly that the famous conjureman had arrived and was about to perform. Neighbors from miles around hustled down the mountain to see the show. The African had been brought there at the point of a gun and with terror in his eyes, but once he began chanting his mumbo-jumbo and swinging his magic glass ball, he was transformed into the master of the moment.

They had started out down by the river, but the conjureman soon led them back up the hill to Frankie's and Charlie's little cabin. Once inside, he kept swinging the glass ball and shuffled about in circles. He went back and forth on the wide puncheon floor boards, one at a time. Suddenly he stopped and shouted in a trance, "HOWJA!" The glass ball stood still at the end of its string. When they took up the board, they found a huge splotch of blood and big chunks of charred flesh still attached to pieces of ribs and thigh bones.

Somebody cried, "That's all that's left of pore ol' Charlie. Whoever done this ought to be in hell with his back broke."

Frankie took one look and fainted dead away. She came to mighty quick when they poured a stiff drink of corn whiskey down her throat. The sheriff had found something else, a rounded piece of iron. "Have ye ever seen this before, Frankie?"

"Yes," she said, "hit's the heel iron off Charlie's hunting boots."

"Well," the sheriff said, "ye might as well confess, Frankie, 'cause we know you done it."

The sheriff said he knew Charlie's body was right there because he knew the dog would have stayed where Charlie was. The sheriff then explained that he had gotten old Jack Collis to poke around the house while everybody else was out searching through the woods and Collis had found the heel iron and all kinds of bone fragments.

Frankie protested all the way across the mountains, 50 miles to the jail and courthouse in Morganton. But the sheriff had the evidence. A grand jury returned an indictment, and Frankie was arraigned. The judge called in 150 people from which a jury was empaneled to hear her case. Hundreds of people poured into the tiny town of Morganton and tried in vain to get into the little courtroom at the old log courthouse.

The prosecutor passed around the deadly axe and pointed out that it had notches made from striking something harder than mere hickory wood. He said that doctors had established that the bits of bone and teeth found in the fireplace were not from wild game but from a human being. The jury and all the folks crowded into the courtroom gasped when one witness said there was a pool of blood under the cabin floor "big as a hog's liver." The Silvers went on the stand to say Frankie had lied about the last time she saw Charlie and about everything else that happened the morning after the crime.

"Charlie come in from chopping wood," said the prosecutor in his summary to the jury, "and then — all innocent of the evil plot in the mind of his nagging, jealous wife — laid down before the fire to play with his little girl and fell asleep, unaware that his wife was at that moment carrying out the deed she'd planned for weeks — months maybe. Her shadow fell across him in the flickerin' glow of the flames. The axe raised high above her head, she summoned a strength born of months of pent-up hatred and…"

"Stop! Stop it!" Frankie screamed. "It's not true. It's not true. It didn't happen that way at'all." But her lawyer, old Nick Woodfin, pulled her back down and told her she couldn't say anything.

The trial went on for days, but finally the jury came in with the verdict: "We, the jury, find the prisoner, Frances Silver, guilty of the felony and murder whereof she stands charged in the bill of indictment."

The crowd gasped at what this meant. If Frankie was guilty, she had to die. One of them burst out, "Kin they hang a woman?" Judge Daniel answered that soon enough by ordering that she be "hung by the neck until dead."

The state supreme court refused to overrule the lower court and Frankie was scheduled to be hanged during the fall superior court. Then one morning in the summer word spread that she had escaped. Her brother made a false key out of wood that would open the locks and let her out of the cell. He had a big wagonload of hay waiting outside and she quickly burrowed under the hay and changed from her prison dress into the man's clothes her brother had brought. She stood in front of him and let him cut off her long blonde hair. She didn't have a lookin' glass to see herself, but Frankie didn't care how she looked; she would have done anything to get out of that stinking cell. Her uncle and brother drove the wagon out of town, and a few miles out, Frankie got down and walked along behind.

Sheriff Boone had a hunch, and he followed the wagon road west. Several miles out from Morganton he could see a wagon with a lone figure walking behind. The sheriff spurred his horse and pulled alongside the young walker.

"Howdy, Frankie!" he said.

"I thank ye, sir, my name's Tommy," she snapped back.

The driver of the wagon had by now stopped to see what was happening. He jumped down and ran over to concur. "Yes, sir, her name's Tommy."

Frankie quickly said, "You want to buy some hay?"

The sheriff said, "No, we don't want any hay, but we do want you, Frankie."

Then the sheriff couldn't stop laughing. "Her name?" he said. "So HER name is Tommy. If that ain't a joke. Frankie, I might not acaught you in all them men's clothes with your hair cut off if this fool uncle of your'un hadn' amade that slip."

The hanging was finally set for July 12, 1833. Morganton was thronged with thousands of people, some said as many as 10,000. The county at that time went clear to the Tennessee border. There had been hangings before, of course, and they were swell occasions, more like a country fair than a solemn ceremony of death.

For the first time in Burke County, hell, in North Carolina, folks were going to get to see a woman put to death. Folks had crowded in around the crude scaffold built of rough pine boards. Frankie was led up to the platform by the sheriff and the hangman. Some people yelled at her for the evil deed she'd done. One man said, "Why, she ain't scared a bit."

Sheriff Boone broke the deathly silence as everybody stood staring at Frankie standing there with the noose dangling over her head: "Frankie, have ye got anything to say?"

The crowd grew tense as everybody leaned in to see if this tough little mountain woman would finally break down and ask forgiveness. Suddenly, from right in front, her daddy yelled:

"Die with it in ye, Frankie."

"Nevermind, Pa," she said looking down, "I'm not afraid."

"Yes," Frankie said to the sheriff, "I have something to say — a lot to say — but I'm going to sing it."

She reached into the folds of her simple homespun dress and pulled out a long, folded piece of paper on which she'd written 15 verses. And then, with a clear unwavering voice, Frankie began to sing the only confession she'd ever make.

This dreadful, dark and dismal day
Has swept my glories all away —
My sun goes down, my days are past
And I must leave this world at last.

The jealous thought that first gave strife
To make me take my husband's life,
For months and days I spent my time
Thinking how to commit this crime.

And on a dark and doleful night
I put his body out of sight,
With flames I tried him to consume
But time would not admit it done.

Ye all see me and on me gaze
Be careful how ye spend thy days
And never commit this awful crime
But try to serve your God in time.

Most folks say this was the way the song about "Frankie and Johnny" got its start. The man's name was really Charlie, and the song would go through all kinds of changes before it got down to the popular song we sing nowadays.

Frankie finished her song and the hangman stepped forward. He pulled a black hood over her head and fit the noose around her neck. He grabbed the latchstring and pulled. The pine boards underneath her fell, and Frankie swung free in death, her pretty neck broken by the rope.

Frankie's family had heard that medical students got the corpses of hanged men and they couldn't bear to think of their Frankie being dissected, well, the way ol' Charlie was. So her daddy dug four separate graves to throw the scavengers off, and then the family set off on the old Yellow Mountain Road toward the steep hills of home. They'd only gotten about eight or nine miles outside town when they stopped at the old Buckhorn Tavern. By the next morning, the stench was overhwelming because the body was rapidly decomposing in the July heat.

A little girl named Nan DeVault followed the little caravan a ways past the old tavern and watched as they pulled off the road and commenced to dig a grave. They opened the casket for one last look at their beautiful daughter and sister; and the little girl watching from the bushes fainted dead away.

It seemed like God had cursed the whole Stewart family because they must have been involved in this horrible crime. Frankie's daddy was cutting down a tree to split for rails when it fell on him and crushed his skull. Her mother died from a rattlesnake bite soon after that. Her brother Blackstone stole a mule and was hanged for it. Her brother Jack was killed in the Civil War.

And even nowadays in those world-lost coves back up in the mountains of North Carolina, the old folks will sit and stare into the fire and smell bacon fat afrying and start to talk about the way poor Charlie Silver was killed by his conniving wife. Some can even sing the song Frankie herself sang — no, it wasn't about Frankie and Johnny, it was about Charlie Silver, a good man who never deserved to die.

It is a powerful story. Unfortunately, almost none of it is true. The true story, the facts, you will discover in the rest of this book, are even more interesting than the story as it has been passed down by so many ballad singers, storytellers and newspaper columnists.

Part II

The Search for Facts about Frankie and Charlie

A Personal Confession
and Some Important Corrections

Now, I would not call everything in Part One of this book a lie. It's just that a lot of us, when we tell a story, we quite naturally fudge a bit, fill in the gaps where we don't know for sure what happened.

I am reminded of the story of an editor asking William Faulkner to straighten out some contradictions and inconsistencies in his novel, The Sound and the Fury. Faulkner came back with a cast of characters as a kind of new preface to the Modern Library edition of his book. His editor gently pointed out that Faulkner had created even more inconsistencies. But, the great author answered: "That's the way you tell a story."

In more recent times, we have the example of young Tom Wolfe (not the one who was born in Asheville, N.C.) watching in amazement when he worked on the old *New York Herald Tribune* as Jimmy Breslin would come back with these absolutely fantastic quotations from all these fascinating characters he seemed to find just walking around New York. Then, it occured to him, "He's fudging it." Wolfe himself went on to a highly profitable career as a proponent of this "New Journalism" and a writer of genuine fiction.

And so, with these rather distinguished precedents, I confess to my own role in passing along some of the misconceptions about the Frankie Silver case. Those lines at the beginning of Part I are from an article I published about Frankie in the May, 1976, *Ms.* magazine. I had borrowed it from Muriel Earley Sheppard's account in her book, *Cabins in the Laurel,* and Lord only knows where she got it. I certainly never heard anybody or even heard about anybody who was set to talking about the way Charlie Silver died whenever he or she smelled bacon fat afrying in the skillet, as I phrased it.

The most chilling moment in my research for this book came when I consulted the bibliography of a thesis written by Carolyn Sakowski in May of 1972 for a master's degree at Appalachian State University. It was a project in historical research and, I might add, one of the most factually correct pieces ever written about Frankie Silver — except for one point. Ms. Sakowski, who is now president of John Blair Publishers in Winston-Salem, N.C., had listed an article about Frankie Silver which I had published in the *Durham Morning Herald* on December 22, 1962. "This source led to Battle's information concerning Woodfin," she wrote about me. Under Kemp P. Battle's book, *Memories of an Old-Time Tar Heel*, Sakowski explains: "This is the only source which suggests that Nick Woodfin was Frankie's lawyer...Since Battle is a reliable historian and he bases his statement on a personal interview with Woodfin, this theory is quite feasible. Because of the unrelated title, it would seem no one but Perry Young of the *Durham Morning Herald* thought to consult it for an answer to the question."

Now, that is nice praise indeed for a piece by the 21-year-old cub reporter I was in 1962. However, it simply wasn't true. Kemp Battle was wrong and I was twice as wrong for repeating his mistake. It is one of the more common errors in the stories that have been published about Frankie Silver, that her lawyer was Nicholas Washington Woodfin of Asheville. In fact, her lawyer was Thomas Worth Wilson who lived in Morganton.

Two other errors are consistently repeated in nearly every article referred to in the bibliography of secondary sources at the end of this book. The worst of these is that Frankie was the first woman, or the only woman, or the only white woman ever hanged in North Carolina. She was none of the above. She was not even the first or only white woman hanged in Burke County.

As recently as November of 1997, the *Durham Morning Herald* and the *Mitchell County News-Journal* both ran stories which described Frankie as the first and only white woman legally hanged in North Carolina. And so did a documentary film, "The Ballad of Frankie Silver," prepared in part by the Folklife Department at the University of North Carolina at Chapel Hill and distributed in video tape in 1997.

The truth is we will never know for sure how many women were executed in North Carolina prior to 1910, when the state took over the administration of all capital punishment in Raleigh. Before that, it was purely a local matter and many of the local court records have been destroyed and some of those that survive are in disarray.

The late Dr. Edward Phifer was for many years the premier historian of Burke County. He was the author of numerous articles and the standard book on Burke County history. Among Phifer's papers in the Southern Historical Collection at Chapel Hill, I found documentation that one and possibly two white women and a third black woman were hanged in Morganton long before the hanging of Frankie Silver.

Phifer wrote a lengthy dissertation on criminal actions in the old Morgan District Superior Court at Morganton from 1782 to 1792. Prior to the establishment of the Morgan District Court at Morganton in 1782, all superior court matters for the western part of the state — including the settlements in what would become Tennessee — were handled in Salisbury District Court in Salisbury. At the time of its formation, Morgan District included Wilkes, Burke, Lincoln and Rutherford in present day North Carolina and Washington and Sullivan in what is now Tennessee. In 1808, the state General Assembly established superior courts in each county and the Morgan District Superior Court was dissolved. In this unpublished paper, Phifer says, "John Wells, yeoman, and Elizabeth, his wife, were indicted and tried in September term, 1788, charged with feloniously burning the dwelling of John Grouse, were both found guilty, and were both sentenced to be executed. They were hanged on 10 October 1788." Along with the typed manuscript, there was a photostat of the original court document that confirmed that Elisabeth (as it is spelled in the original) Wells and her husband were hanged on October 10, 1788.

After I had written the above, I wondered if, in fact, John and Elisbeth Wells were tried and hanged at Morganton, since the crime had taken place in Lincoln County. That was when I discovered the following in Weyette Haun's four volume transcription (from microfilm) of all the surviving records of the Morgan District Court now in the state archives in Raleigh:

"State of North Carolina Morgan District Superior Court October 21st 1788. The State vs. John Wells & Elisabeth Wells. Indictment Arson. Jury impannelled & Sworn viz: Thomas Wheeler, Samuel Lusk, Francis McCorkle, Thomas Kell, Jonathan Hampton, Thomas Bradburn, Thomas Young, William Bealy, Joseph Herndon, William Grant, William Thruston, William T. Lewis. The jury find John Wells and Elisabeth Wife of the said John, Prisoners at the Bar, Guilty of the Felony and house burning whereof they stand charged in manner and form as charged in the bill of Indictment. I hereby certify that the said Malefactors (to wit) John Wells and Elisabeth his wife were hanged agreeable to the order and Sentence of the Superior Court of Law on the Tenth day of October Instant. Given under my hand at office the 27th day of October Anno Domini 1788 Wm. Erwin Clk. State Vs. John Wells & Elisabeth his wife."

Still, this entry did not say the trial and hanging took place at Morganton, so I looked further. One of the jurors, Thomas Young, you see, was my great, great, great grandfather and I know that his house stood where Honeycutt Creek comes into the North Fork of the Catawba River in the North Cove of what is now McDowell County. The site was and is roughly 20 miles from Morganton which would mean a 40-mile round trip. In the miscellaneous court records transcribed by Haun, I found the following: "State of North Carolina Morgan District Septr. term 1788 Superior Court of Law, Thomas Young charges as juror to 11 days attendance." My ancestor was paid 4 pounds, 19 shillings and 4 pence for serving on this jury and the bill states he had traveled "40 miles to court and home." If that was not enough proof, I found further evidence in these same miscellaneous records that "John Wells was executed at Morganton and has no property in this county nor any county in this state as I can find. Joseph Henry, Sherif of Lincoln County October 24th 1789."

In yet another capital case Phifer discovered, one Margaret Smith was indicted for murder at the September 1782 Morgan District Court. She was accused of killing her infant child on December 26, 1780. Phifer could not find out whether Smith was ever tried and convicted and hanged. And there is no reference to this case in Haun's books. However, in a study of the dispositions of similar cases in nearby Rowan County for the same period, Phifer found that everybody indicted for murder was convicted and hanged.

His own research notwithstanding, Phifer went on to say in his published history of Burke County: "Frankie is believed to have been the only free white female to be hanged in the county at any time in its history. At least one female slave, Betsey, who belonged to John McTaggart, was hanged in the summer of 1813 after being judged guilty in County Court of serving as an accomplice in the murder of her master."

According to the Capital Punishment Research Project at the University of Alabama School of Law in Tuscaloosa, Alabama, at least 13 women are known to have been executed in North Carolina prior to 1910, and this list does not include the three women mentioned above. The race of two of the women was not known, but of those whose race was known, only two were white. According to this list, the first white woman hanged in North Carolina was Caroline Sullivan, who was hanged in Edenton in 1738 or 1739. The second white woman on this list is Frankie Silver, who was hanged in 1833 in Burke County. The others are either all black or their race was not known to the researchers in Alabama. Many were burned at the stake, but one, a slave named Margaritte, was hanged in Yanceyville in 1828, five years before Frankie.

Caroline Shipp was believed to have been the last woman hanged in North Carolina. According to a story in *The Charlotte Observer* of December 26, 1979, she was hanged on December 18, 1896 (the Alabama researchers list the hanging in 1892). *The Observer* reported: "Miss Shipp, who was the last woman hanged in North Carolina, sang songs and ate her last meal of sardines and crackers.

"Shortly after 8 a.m., a horse pulling the buckboard that carried the coffin arrived at a huge oak tree that still stands near a pauper's graveyard a few yards from the prison camp. (The camp is still a prison unit.)

"Van Sellers, who lived near Cherryville, kicked a wooden box from under Miss Shipp, who fell about 2 feet before the rope stopped her fall.

"But the jolt didn't break her neck. Miss Shipp's weight wasn't enough to snap her spinal column. A man stepped from the crowd that had gathered and pulled at her feet until she died."

The next paragraph of *The Charlotte Observer* story points up the crying need for further research in this vitally important area. Once a mistake gets into the clipping files of newspapers it gets repeated every time a fresh young reporter "goes to the files" and refers to the misstatement of fact. Hear what the *Observer* had to say about Frankie Silver in this story: "Caroline Shipp had been convicted of murder. She was one of two women hanged in North Carolina history. The other, Frankie Silver, was hanged in 1833. Her hometown couldn't be determined."

Since the state took over the job of administering capital punishment only three women have actually been executed. Bessie Mae Williams, a black housekeeper convicted of the murder of a taxi driver in Mecklenburg County, died in the gas chamber on December 29, 1944; Roseanna Lightner Phillips, a black housemaid who was convicted of murder in Durham County, was executed on January 1, 1943; Velma Barfield was executed on November 2, 1984, by lethal injection for the poisoning death of her boyfriend. (She had admitted killing her mother and two elderly people in her care as well, but was never tried for their deaths.).

The third major mistake that is repeated in most, but not, all of the books and articles about Frankie Silver is that from the gallows she read or sang a confessional poem she had written. The true history of "The Ballad of Frankie Silver" is in Part III of this book.

In Part I, I should add, I relied very heavily on one of the most sensational accounts — complete with dialogue — ever published about Frankie Silver. This was an article by Robert Menzies and Edmond Smith published in the July 1935 issue of *True Detective Mysteries* magazine. It is found inside a lurid cover advertising another story, "The Nude Beauty." Frankie's story was called "The Scarlet Enigma of Toe River."

We can assume that the dialogue is pure fiction and so are a number of the names used, such as "Zeb Cranberry." However, there are some tantalizing facts that these authors seem to have uncovered — such as the name of the slavemaster who owned a Guinea conjureman in Tennessee — and I'd love to know who they were and what their sources were. Unfortunately, I could find nobody who knew of them and there are no references to either of them in the major North Carolina historical collections. Most of the historical information in the article, however, is as fictitious as the dialogue. They call Charles Silver's father, John Silver. Well, the man's name was Jacob Silver, a fact of history. But because their article got into the clipping files at newspapers and in the historical files at libraries, Jacob became John to Manley Wade Wellman and dozens of other authors who followed with articles about Frankie Silver.

It is in that spirit — that I am partly to blame but would like to make amends for my mistakes — that I hope this book will be read, especially from this point on. The study of history is an ongoing process and correcting the mistakes of the past is a vital part of that process. The problem with local history is that too much of it is written too quickly and often from news clips and files that are themselves full of mistakes. I hope from this point I will show that with a little more time and research you can come up with a much more interesting story.

Chronology

December 22, 1831	Charles Silver is killed by his wife, Frances.
January 9, 1832	A murder warrant is issued for the arrest of Frankie Silver, her mother, Barbara Stuart, and her brother, Blackstone Stuart.
January 10, 1832	All three are jailed in Morganton.
January 13, 1832	Frankie's father gets a writ of habeas corpus and demands an immediate hearing before a magistrate, saying his wife, daughter and son are being unlawfully detained.
January 17, 1832	A hearing is held and charges are dropped against Barbara Stuart and Blackstone Stuart; Frankie is held in jail.
March 17, 1832	Spring term of Burke Superior Court begins. Frankie is indicted for murder. Charges against her mother and brother are formally dismissed.
March 29, 1832	Frankie's trial is held and jury retires "about candlelight."
March 30, 1832	Jurors report they are deadlocked nine to three for acquittal and ask for re-examination of certain witnesses. Afterward, they return a unanimous verdict of guilt. Judge Donnell sentences Frankie to be hanged in July 1832. Her lawyer gives notice of appeal.

May 3, 1832	Under the rules of the time, Judge Donnell files the appeal.
June term, 1832	The North Carolina Supreme Court rejects the appeal and orders the sentence of death to be carried out at the fall term of Burke Superior Court.
September, 1832	Judge David L. Swain is severely injured in a fall from his sulky so there is no fall term of court in Burke County and Frankie's execution is put off until the spring term. Swain is subsequently elected governor by the General Assembly to replace Montfort Stokes who has resigned to become Indian Commissioner in what is now Arkansas and Oklahoma.
March, 1833	At the spring term of Burke Superior Court, Frankie's execution date is set for June 28.
May 18, 1833	Frankie escapes from jail.
May 26, 1833	Frankie is apprehended in Rutherford County and brought back to jail. Her father, uncle and one other unidentified man are jailed for helping her escape.
June, 1833	Governor Swain grants a two-week reprieve for Frankie to "prepare herself" for death.
July 12, 1833	Frances Stuart Silver is hanged.

The Setting

Even now the place where Charles Silver was killed is a remote and isolated spot. A two-lane blacktop road meanders up and around and over the steep mountains on the border of Yancey and Mitchell counties to a place called Kona, near the North Carolina-Tennessee border.

The old folks all referred to the area as Toe River, but in more recent years, an engineer at the feldspar processing plant gave the community an official new name from the chemical elements of feldspar — K for potassium, O for oxygen and Na for sodium. The swift waters of the Toe River cut around the base of the mountains in deep horseshoe bends, but there's almost no level land that could honestly be called a valley. To get there nowadays, you take NC 80 north from US-19E and cross the North Toe River at Newdale. Then you wind up and over the mountainside and down again to a picturesque old one-lane arched concrete bridge across the river, and then you wind up and around still more mountains and down to Kona and again to the swift river's edge.

Difficult as the journey is, your reward is coming around a high bend in the road and suddenly seeing this historic mountain community spread out around two beautiful old white churches commanding two gentle hilltops. I have made the journey many times myself, just one among hundreds who come here every year for two very different reasons: it is the ancestral home of the Silver family which is now spread throughout the United States; and it is the site of one of the most bizarre murders in the history of Appalachia.

In more recent years, there has been a fanciful tale that the name "Toe" comes from an Indian legend about a star-crossed romance that left an

Indian maiden named Estatoe heartbroken. She drowned herself in the river and gave it her name, which was shortened to Toe. In fact, the only Estatoe mentioned in Cherokee records was not a maiden, but the "warrior prince of Estatoe."

A more reliable early account says the river was named by the area's first European settler, Hunting John McDowell. McDowell had been granted land along the Catawba River at the foot of the Blue Ridge by Lord Granville as early as 1754 when it was in Anson County of the royal colony. He named any number of geographic points — such as Table Rock and Humpback mountains — and all of them were descriptive. It was not the "Toe" but the "Tow" River he named, doubtless because of its swift current, or tow, and that is how the name is spelled in all the early records.

It was surely the very rugged nature of the land that brought the Silvers and Stewarts into this area. The flat, bottom land had all been taken and granted to the first settlers 40 and 50 years earlier; the only free government land left was the steep hillsides that had been passed over by others. In its day, the area was as impenetrable as the thickest jungles in the rainforests.

It is impossible now to imagine the rough life the first settlers had quite literally cutting their way through laurel thickets and trying to clear the dense forests and build a homestead on the steep terrain. There was no such thing as a road. They were lucky if there was even an animal trail wide enough for a man and a horse to get through.

The Silvers

George Silber Sr. was part of that vast migration of Protestants who came to America in the 1720s from the warring Catholic and Protestant kingdoms and principalities that now comprise the nation of Germany. He is believed to have settled in Pennsylvania, where his son, George Jr. was born in 1751. The name was soon anglicized to Silver.

At some point, George Silver Jr. moved on down to Fredericktown, Maryland, which he listed as his home when he enlisted in revolutionary service for six months at Annapolis. He re-enlisted for 18 months "in the Flying Camp" and was wounded in the Battle of Germantown, when a bullet grazed the skin of his neck. He enlisted a third time, for three years service "in the German regiment." He fought against Cornwallis at Yorktown and served under General Greene in South Carolina until the end of the war, when he was marched back to Maryland and discharged.

George Silver Jr. married Ann, or Nancy (both names appear in family records) Griffith on April 12, 1782. She was the eighth of 10 children of Orlando and Elizabeth Griffith. The Griffiths had arrived in Maryland in 1675 and were among the colony's wealthiest landowners, having married into the Duvall, Howard, and Greenberry families. Nicholas Greenberry was the keeper of the great seal in Colonial Maryland and his surname endured as a given name for 200 years among the emigrants from Maryland to North Carolina. Two of Ann Griffith Silver's older brothers, Zadock and Chisholm, moved to Buncombe and Rowan Counties in North Carolina in the early 1800s.

There is a family tradition that George and Ann Silver and their 11 children, along with her brothers, John and William Griffith, and a family named Ellis came in a wagon train from Maryland in 1806. According to an early Griffith family history, the children of George and Ann Griffith Silver were: 1. John Silver, born in 1786; 2. George Silver, born in 1788; 3. Elizabeth Silver, born in 1790; 4. Sarah Silver, born in 1792; 5. Jacob Silver, born in 1793; 6. Greenberry Silver, born in February of 1795; 7. Rachel Silver, born in 1796; 8. William Silver, born in 1798; 9. Henry Silver, born in 1800; 10. Nancy Silver, born in 1802; and 11. Thomas Silver, born in 1804.

Jacob Silver's first wife is believed to have been named Elizabeth Wilson. According to family legend, she died during the birth of her first and only child, the ill-fated Charles Silver. This curious notation is in the Silver family Bible: "Born to Jacob in Morganton by his first wife whose name no one remembers, Charles Silver, born October 3, 1812 — Slain by his wife, Frankie, December 1831." Since the Bible was not printed until 1849, all of the family records were written long after the actual birthdates transcribed, but this particular note appears to be even more recent.

Although family tradition has it that Jacob and his father moved into the Toe River Valley in 1806, it could have been later. George and Ann Silver were still in Maryland as late as 1802, when they signed papers regarding her Griffith inheritance. In his claim for a military pension, at age 80 in 1872, Jacob Silver said he enlisted in the North Carolina militia in 1813 and served until he was discharged November 15, 1815. He had been called into federal service on February 17, 1815, the day after the peace treaty was ratified ending the War of 1812.

The earliest land grant to Jacob Silver in North Carolina was dated 1818. The family says he had entered the land long before that and only registered it when others started encroaching on what he considered his property. The father and son built a huge two-story log house which still stands, nestled in a protective cove below the old churches at Kona. It followed the classic frontier model. There were two large rooms with enormous stone chimneys and fireplaces at either end. In between these rooms was an open "dog trot." An attic, or sleeping loft, ran across all three spaces. By 1997, for sale signs began appearing around the property. Until that time, however, the house and 100 acres around it had never been bought, sold, mortgaged or insured — and had always been lived in by a direct descendant of the Revolutionary soldier who is buried up on the hill.

After his first wife died, Jacob Silver was married on October 6, 1814 to Nancy, the daughter of Samuel Reed, or Reid, in Buncombe County. Jacob and Nancy Reed Silver had 12 children, nine sons and three daughters: 1.

Margaret "Peggy" Silver was born December 2, 1815, and married Mitchell Robinson. She died May 26, 1909 at the age of 93 and is buried in the old family cemetery; 2. Alfred L. Silver was born November 15, 1816 and first married Elizabeth Gouge, second Sarah E. Chandler. He died September 10, 1905, at the age of 88 and is buried at Old Fort. 3. John Silver was born July 13, 1818, and according to family tradition was a devout Christian who took on his younger brother Marvel's illness and died himself at age 18. 4. Milton Silver was born February 2, 1820 and died in 1839 of typhoid fever. 5. Rachel Silver was born December 15, 1821, and married William M. Robinson. She died February 6, 1866, at the age of 63. 6. Lucinda "Cindy" Silver was born February 3, 1826, and married Wilborn Norman. She died March 24, 1927, at the age of 101. 7. Marvel Alexander Silver was born December 11, 1827, and died May 1, 1838. 8. William Jacob "Billy" Silver was born November 9, 1829, and married Sarah Ann Patton. He died May 19, 1878, at the age of 48. 9. David Ralph Silver was born February 21, 1832, and married first Elizabeth Baker, second Sarah Ledford, and third Rosannah Wilson Gouge. He died August 26, 1911, at the age of 79. 10. Samuel Marion "Colonel Sam" Silver was born December 30, 1833, and married first Mary Anne Wilson, second Martha Anne Young [my great aunt] and third Amanda Emmaline Ray. He died on May 7, 1922, at the age of 88 and is buried in Troy, Oregon. 11. Reuben Silver was born August 4, 1836, and married Sarah Ann Sparks. He was killed by lightning while looking for a bee tree on June 14, 1859, when he was 23 years old. 12. Edmund Drury Silver was born September 14, 1838, and married Arzilla E. Payne. He died March 28, 1910, in Grouse, Oregon, from injuries he got from being thrown from a mule.

(Dear reader, please do not think that I am wasting your time with all these names and dates. Most will occur later in the story and the way many of these family members died is an important footnote to a later accusation.)

In his pension application, Jacob Silver is described as a very stout man, six feet tall, with dark hair, black eyes and fair complexion. He preached at several Baptist churches in the Toe River area for more than 50 years. Family legend has it that although he could not read and write, his wife would read the scripture to him and he would memorize it for his sermons. However, when Nancy Reed Silver applied for a widow's pension when she was 83 year old, she signed with an X.

Alfred Silver has left us a delightful description of his older half-brother, Charles: "He was strong and healthy, good looking and agreeable. He had lots of friends. Everybody liked him. He was a favorite at all the parties for he could make merry by talking, laughing and playing musical instruments. I think he was the best fifer that I ever heard."

In an interview with H.E.C. "Red Buck" Bryant, published in *The Charlotte Observer* in 1903, Alfred Silver also described his late sister-in-law, Frankie. He said she "was a mighty likely little woman. She had fair skin, bright eyes, and was counted very pretty. She had charms. I never saw a smarter little woman. She could card and spin her three yards of cotton a day on a big wheel."

Of all the later accounts of the story of Frankie and Charlie, Alfred Silver's seems the most reliable. He was just four years younger than Charles and he was a young man at the very impressionable age of 15 when the murder took place just a quarter mile across the ridge from the family home where he lived. By contrast, in her book, *Cabins in the Laurel*, Muriel Early Sheppard relies on an account given her by W.W. Bailey of Spruce Pine who said he got it from Charle's half sister, Cindy Silver Norman. Cindy Silver was only five years old when the murder took place.

The Stewarts

Frankie had been brought into the mountains as a young girl with her family. Her mother, Barbara or Barbary, listed her birthdate as 1778 and her own birthplace as Virginia in the 1850 census, but I was not able to find out who her parents were. She did name one of her sons Blackstone, an old Virginia surname. She ended up living in Anson County, N.C., and married to Isaiah Stewart. Although the family now spells the name Stewart, it was generally spelled Stuart or Stuard in the early deeds and the records of Frankie's trial. Except when quoting documents, I will use the modern spelling. Apparently neither Isaiah nor Barbara could read or write since all of the surviving records they signed are signed with an X.

(I am grateful to Dan W. Olds of Spartanburg, S.C., for the detailed information on the Stewart family, his wife's ancestors. There is also a national organization of the family which publishes a newsletter called The Stewart Clan, from which some of this information was taken.)

Isaiah was the son of William and Priscilla Stewart. William Stewart's will, dated November 25, 1816, was probated in January, 1817. In it, he named the following children: Joseph, John, Isaiah, William, Phebe, Delilah, Frances, Mary. Frankie was thus named for her aunt. In the 1820 census, Murdoch, William and Isaiah Stewart are listed as living south of Richardson's Creek in Anson County. Isaiah's household included two males under 10, one 10-15, one 16-18, two 16-25, and one over 44, one female under 10 (presumably Frances), and one 26-44.

From the records, it appears that Isaiah and his family left Anson County for the mountains in the mid-1820s. On March 18, 1823, he sold 175 acres adjoining Jackson Stewart to Charles Stewart. On November 15, 1825, he

31

sold another 155 acres in Anson County to William Stewart. By 1830, Isaiah or "Ice" Stewart is a resident of Buncombe County in the mountains, where he was a witness to a deed from Charles to Nathan Stewart. Although Isaiah Stewart's name does not appear in the grantor or grantee index in Buncombe, the family apparently moved into a cove just across the ridge from where the Silver family had settled about 20 years earlier. It is still known as Stewart's Cove.

The area was first in Anson County, created for all of western North Carolina in 1750, and then in Rowan when that county was created in 1753. After independence, the mountain people wanted a county seat closer than Salisbury and Burke was created in 1777 with Morganton as its seat. The area then became part of Buncombe in 1791 and part of Yancey in 1833 and finally of Mitchell County in 1861.

The 1830 census for Burke County lists the family of Isaiah Stewart. He and his wife are listed under the column for 40-50- year-olds, and there is one male 10-15 and two females 15-20. Dan Olds got the following list of children of Isaiah and Barbara Stewart from Chandler Stewart, the great-grandson of their son Joseph. The children of Isaiah and Barbara Stewart: 1. John C. Stewart was born March 9, 1800, and died February 22, 1893. He married Mahaly Gurley, who was born June 15, 1810, and died June 15, 1909. 2. Jackson Stewart was born August 18, 1807, and died November 12, 1864. He married Elizabeth Howell, who lived from 1808 to 1888. 3. Joseph Stewart was born December 12, 1813, and died March 31, 1863. He married Elizabeth Gibbs Finley. 4. Blackstone Stewart was born in 1817. In the 1850 census, his wife is listed as Levinia, age 33, and his children as Berry, 10, Joseph, 7, and Louisa E., 12. 5. Frances Stewart was born around 1810 and was hanged on July 12, 1833. 6. Jacob Stewart is also listed as a possible son of Isaiah by Chandler Stewart although his name does not appear in any of the records relating to Frankie's trial. 7. Charles Stewart is listed in several documents with Isaiah Stewart, although the relationship is not spelled out. A Charles Stewart is listed in the 1830 and 1840 Burke County census, which suggests he did not move across the mountains into what would have become Yancey County by the latter date.

Frankie and Charlie

Like most of their neighbors, the Stewarts and Silvers were poor people who had taken this rugged land nobody else wanted and managed to eke out a living for their families.

Charles Silver and Frankie Stewart were only 17 or 18 years old when they married in 1829, or 1830. One assumes they were formally married — like Charles' parents and grandparents — although it was not uncommon in those days so far from any town or church for young couples to just "take up housekeeping together." Many of the Burke County marriage records for that time were destroyed and there is no mention in any family Bible of their marriage.

Charles' father gave him a piece of land across the ridge and that is where he and Frankie built their little cabin. When I first visited the site in the 1960s, a few foundation logs still lay among the crumbled ruins of the old rock fireplace and chimney. It had been a one-room cabin, made of hewn logs. What struck me was an unusual feature for a rough cabin in such a mean place. Out front were enormous old boxwoods 15 feet high. I couldn't help but wonder if they hadn't been planted by a young girl named Frankie with dreams of making a happier life in that rough setting.

On November 3, 1830, Frankie gave birth to her first and only child. She was named Nancy, surely for Charles' grandmother, or possibly for his step-mother who was also named Nancy. Both George and Nancy Griffith Silver were still alive. He would not die until 1839, she until 1849.

If the land proved a difficult place to raise the kind of food and fodder crops taken for granted in the flatlands, it was still mostly a wilderness rich in a vast array of wild game and berries and medicinal herbs. The first settlers on this mountain frontier did not raise what they ate, they hunted it. Alfred Silver recalled, "Charles was pretty much of a gunner, a hunter."

We have only Alfred's words about what happened to Charlie on December 22, 1831. Although Frankie did give a full confession before she was hanged and it was written down, no copy of this confession has yet been found.

Alfred Silver recalled: "The ground was all covered with snow and the river was frozen hard. His wife, contending that he would be off soon on a hunt, urged him to cut enough wood to do all week. He fell in with his axe and cut up a whole hickory tree, and shocked it so that it would keep, dry and clean.

"Being tired and sleepy after the labor of chopping, my brother lay down on the floor, close by the fire with his little girl in his arms, and went to sleep. His head rested on an inverted stool for a pillow. Franky gently took the baby from his breast, put it to bed, picked up the axe from the door, where she had placed it for the purpose, and whacked his head half off at a single blow. She intended to cut it clean off, but miscalculated and either stood too close or too far back. The first lick did not kill him instantly for he sprang to his feet and cried: 'God bless the child!' The wife fled to the bed by the child, and covered herself up, 'til she heard Charles fall, then jumped out and finished the job with a second blow."

Now, how Alfred Silver was supposed to have come up with such specific eye-witness details from a quarter mile away is anybody's guess.

It is a fact that the idea that Charlie was killed while he lay sleeping dates from the time of the crime. The most obvious explanation is that people simply didn't believe a woman would have the strength to take on such a sturdy outdoorsman and best him in a hand-to-hand fight. She had to sneak up and hit him when he couldn't strike back. In one of the later petitions to the governor, her neighbors said, "We the undersigned believe that the circumstances which are supposed to have attended this murder are so totally inconsistent with human nature that the greatest exertion of female fortitude could not possible [sic] have accomplished the horrid deed." This, of course, does not take into account that the work of women in that time was just as strenuous as anything the men did.

One story has been published claiming that Charles had gone across the river to buy his Christmas liquor from George Young, my great, great uncle, and came home drunk and passed out. I'll vow the Youngs were among the first merchants in the mountains and certainly weren't averse to selling whiskey or anything else they could trade for a buck — or a chicken or a dozen eggs. And, Alfred's description of Charlie certainly fits the image of a man who liked his whiskey. When mountain folk spoke of "making merry," it generally meant whiskey was involved.

Frankie's own lawyer, Thomas W. Wilson, would later write the governor: "It was argued by many, the solicitor too, that she must have killed him while lying asleep by the fire, which was surely possible. He went from his father's near dark perfectly cool & sober in the dead of winter — the house was very open — I lay it is not probable that he would have lain down to sleep by the fire."

Wilson also raised the possibility that Frankie did not act alone. He wrote the governor, "It is believed by many that her parents were very instrumental in the perpetration of that horrid deed." There is a tradition among the Silvers that Frankie's father stood beside her and said, "If you don't kill him I will."

The ostensible reason for the Stewarts being involved in the killing was that they wanted to move west and Charles would not let Frankie go. If so, the facts remain that there was not enough evidence to indict any of the Stewarts except for Frankie — and, after Charlie was long gone, the Stewarts did not move West, but stayed right where they were living. Frankie's lawyer no doubt got it right when he wrote, "She must have killed him by some unlikely blow not premeditated." And he certainly had access to more reliable information than anybody has had since the crime was committed.

Although no copy of Frankie's confession has been found, we do know from several sources that she said her husband had abused her and that she claimed he was loading his gun to kill her when she killed him in self defense.

The Silvers, naturally, swear to this day that their Charlie was a man of sober character who would never lay a hand on his wife. However, the records from that time reveal that most people understood he was not that at all. In the first news report of the crime, published under the headline "Horrible Outrage" in *The North Carolina Spectator & Western Advertiser* in Rutherfordton, January 28, 1832, Charles Silver was said to have been "a man of rather vagrant and intemperate habits." The story also said that Frankie had told several people she would kill him.

"He Treated Her
with Personal Violence"

In the first of the later petitions to the governor, it was stated: "The only inducement on the part of the defendant for the commission of the alleged offense was that of brutal conduct of the husband toward the wife — as appeared in evidence." Spousal abuse was, of course, a way of life at that time in the United States and the rest of the world. Women could not vote, hold public office or serve on juries. Married women had virtually no rights at all; they couldn't even hold property in their own names. The phrase, "rule of thumb" is supposed to come from an English common law tradition that it was all right for a man to beat his wife so long as the stick was no larger than his thumb.

A news item from the *Fayetteville Journal* reprinted in the *Raleigh Star* for September 23, 1830, says it all: "Marital Rights. In our Court of Pleas and Quarter Sessions, which set last week, a man was indicted and tried for whipping his wife. The assault and battery were proven by the oath of the wife and another woman. The husband admitted the battery, but justified himself on the ground that the wife habitually disobeyed his orders, and was in the violation of his commands when the battery complained of was committed. The jury acquitted the defendant. Wives take warning!"

The petitioners for Frankie knew what they were talking about when they said a wife was seldom found guilty of killing her husband, "whilst it has so frequently happened that husbands have murdered their wives and escaped punishment...."

The very same year Frankie Silver killed her husband, a man named Reuben Southard beat his wife to death with a ramrod in Burke County. The gory testimony of several people who witnessed Southard's abuse of

Matilda English Southard and testified at the inquest on October 24, 1831, is preserved in the North Carolina Archives.

"I saw him beat her with a stick on the head.... I saw him beat her with a gun stick.... I saw him beat her with a ramrod.... Joseph England states her face was blacked, that Reuben had done it in a drunken frolick.... He saw Reuben slap her on the face and the blood run from down his knife.... After that, he saw her spit up blood and corruption...."

The jury of inquest found just cause and Reuben was tried, apparently before a magistrates court, the next day with the following verdict: "Whereas it appears to us from Evidence that the Defendant is guilty Judgment is granted against him for three dollars sixty cents cost given under our hands and seals October 25, 1831."

The most explicit information about Charles Silver is preserved in the last-minute and futile effort by the ladies of Morganton to get Frankie pardoned. Since the petition itself was written at the request of Frankie's father, it is safe to assume that the ladies' source of information was not just Frankie's confession, but her father's words as well. The ladies told the governor: "We do not expect to refer you to any information in this that you are not already familiarly acquainted with unless it be the treatment of the unfortunate Creature received during the life of husband.

"We do not refer you to this with a view of justification but merely to reiterate the various unfortunate events that have taken place in the world in consequence of ill grounded abuse indecorous and insupportable treatment in which the creature now before your Excellency for mercy has contrary to the Law of God and the Country yet so consistent with our nature been her own avenger.

"The husband of the unfortunate creature now before you we are informed, Sir, was one of that cast of mankind who are wholly dissolute of any of the feeling that is necessary to make a good Husband or parent — the neighborhood people are Convinced that his treatment to her was both unbecoming and cruel very often and at the time too when female Delicacy would most forbid it. He treated her with personal violence. He was said by all the neighborhood to have been a man who never made use of any exertions to Support either his wife or child which terminated as is frequently the case that those dutys Nature ordered and intended the Husband to perform were thrown to her. His own relatives admit of his having been a lazy trifling man. It is also admitted by them also that she was an industrious woman...."

She Killed Him in Self Defense

While we will never know exactly how Charles Silver was murdered, we do know from at least two men — Henry Spainhour and Nicholas Woodfin — who were in Morganton at the time of the trial that Frankie herself claimed that she killed him in self defense.

In a letter to the *Morganton Star* of May 7, 1886, Henry Spainhour wrote from Lowell, Garrard County, Kentucky, to correct an impression given in an earlier newspaper that Frankie had delivered her "confession" in verse form from the gallows. (This is dealt with in more detail in Part III of this book.) In fact, Spainhour wrote, Frankie "said that Silvers was loading his gun to kill her and she took the ax and struck him on the head and knocked him down, and he seemed to suffer so awfully that she thought it would be mercy of her to kill him."

Henry Spainhour is one of the more interesting and honorable people involved in the Frankie Silver case. He was born in Burke County, July 23, 1809, one of 12 children of Peter Spainhour. Apprenticed as a cabinet — and coffin — maker at an early age, he worked in a shop near the courthouse in Morganton. He wrote, "I was living in Morganton, when she killed her husband and until she was hanged, right in fair view of the place where I was at work, I had a chance to know about all the circumstances."

In 1839, Spainhour married Eliza Beck and they moved to Kentucky. Although he had no truck with the hypocrisy and turmoil of organized religions, Spainhour was a devoutly religious man, his beliefs coming closest to that of the Quakers. He was a fervent opponent of slavery and voted for Abraham Lincoln in 1860. This caused his Confederate neighbors to drive him and his family from their home. They moved to a farm in Illinois but returned after the war, and Henry Spainhour immediately made friends of his former enemies "for he loved all mankind." He died at the ripe age of 92, February 11, 1901, much beloved by all his neighbors.

It was righteous indignation that had caused him to write to the newspaper 53 years after Frankie Silver's death to set the record straight. "I consider it wrong to brand the dead with greater crimes than we believe they were guilty of," he wrote, a noble sentiment which inspires the author of this present book.

Nicholas Woodfin, the only other source that Frankie killed in self defense, was the political and religious opposite to Spainhour. He was born January 29, 1810, a poor farm boy in the Mills River section of Henderson county. (The great Atlanta newspaperman, Henry Woodfin Grady, was the grandson of his mother's younger brother, who was also raised on this farm.) The fourth of 12 children, Woodfin would walk into Asheville to study law under Michael Francis and David Lowry Swain, a lawyer who would become a superior court judge and later governor of the state and president of the university from 1835 until 1867. By the time of the Civil War, Woodfin was a convert to the stylish Episcopal Church and owned property valued at $165,000, including 121 slaves, the largest number owned by anybody in Buncombe County.

Woodfin was licensed to practice law in the superior courts of North Carolina on February 4, 1832, a mere matter of weeks before the trial of Frankie Silver began at Morganton. He was not Frankie's lawyer, although he must have been a spectator at the trial who believed until his death she should never have been hanged.

However, for most of this century, newspaper columnists and local historians have mistakenly identified Woodfin as the lawyer for Frankie Silver, because he was named as such in Kemp P. Battle's *Memories of an Old-Time Tar Heel*. It is well to keep in mind that Battle, former president of the university, began writing his memoirs on his 81st birthday, December 19, 1912, 80 years after Frankie's trial. Battle's son, William James Battle, inherited the manuscript at his father's death, July 3, 1929. He edited the manuscript (for publication by the UNC Press in 1945) because it was full of repetitions and "there were slips both in facts and in style." Battle not only had the wrong lawyer, he also incorrectly stated that Frankie was the only white woman ever hanged in North Carolina.

However, I do think there are some grains of truth in what Battle wrote because they can be corroborated with the memories of Henry Spainhour:

"Not long before his death, I asked him (Woodfin) about the case. He replied earnestly in substance, 'She was unjustly hung. Her story was reasonable and told with every evidence of sincerity. Her husband came home drunk and began to beat her with a stick; she struck back and killed him. She did not intend to kill him, but only to keep him from beating her.'"

Hiding the Evidence

As if Charlie's murder itself were not bad enough, Alfred Silver revealed, "The most atrocious deed was to come. The woman went to work, cut the body into small pieces and burned it bit by bit. The entire night and all the wood available were consumed in burning the body. The hickory tree, a dog house and the door steps went up in the effort."

It seems likely that if Frankie's family members were not involved in the actual killing, they may well have helped dispose of the evidence. Alfred maintained that her mother and younger brother aided in hiding the evidence. "In fact, she (Frankie) confessed as much to a woman who called on her in jail. I believe the killing was a conspiracy entered into by the whole Stewart family."

There is a logical explanation for Frankie's acts. Henry Spainhour wrote, "She was struck with terror, knowing that she would be hung unless she could conceal him, upon which she concluded to burn him."

Nicholas Woodfin told Battle: "She tried to hide the body by cutting it up and burying it."

However logical, it is this gruesome aspect of the case that has caused its fame. It is one thing to shoot and kill your husband; it is quite another to sit by the fire burning him "bit by bit."

Once again, Alfred Silver is our best source on what happened after Charles was killed. The murder took place on December 22, and it would be 18 days before a warrant was issued for Frankie's arrest on January 9, 1832. Almost as hideous as the act itself is the image of the family finding bits and pieces of their oldest son and brother hidden about the place. There are three graves in the old cemetery which, according to family tradition, contain various parts of Charlie. His family was too superstitious to open a grave, so they kept digging new ones as they found different parts of Charlie.

Alfred said that Frankie came over to the Silver place very early the morning after the murder and found his mother and sisters doing the family wash for Christmas.

"You are hard at it early," Frankie said.

"Yes," answered Mrs. Silver, "we are trying to get ready for a rest."

Frankie said she'd been at it since before day. She said Charles had gone across the river to George Young's. That afternoon, she came back to the Silvers' house and said Charles had still not come home and she was going to stay with her parents about three quarters of a mile away.

Charles' younger brothers went to feed the cow and saw only women's tracks in the snow.

The next day Frankie came back and told the Silvers that Charlie still hadn't come home and she didn't care whether he ever came back again. She returned to her parents' house and apparently never came back to the scene of the crime.

The original news report in the *Rutherfordton Spectator & Western Advertiser* of January 28, 1832 corroborates much of what Alfred told*The Charlotte Observer*: "His wife went to the house of her husband, saying that he was not to be found at home, etc. She was told in reply that he had been seen in the afternoon of the preceding day passing towards his own house, and had not been seen since by them. Hereupon, the family set off and tracked him (there being at that time a slight snow on the ground) to home; but no track could be found to proceed from the house in any direction. The woods and river were searched by the neighbors, but without success. In the meantime, the wife had packed up her effects and removed to the house of some neighbor."

Meanwhile, the Silvers started searching the mountains. They looked along the river because some people said maybe he fell in the ice; they went to George Young's house and he said Charlie hadn't been there. Charles' father was beside himself with worry. He set out in the bitter cold on a 40-mile hike across the treacherous mountains to locate a Guinea conjureman he'd heard about in Tennessee who could divine things by using some sort of ball.

The black man wasn't home, but his white master, whose name was Williams, was and he said he also knew how to use the conjure ball. He hung the ball on a string like a pendulum and marked off the points of the compass. The ball didn't move. Williams asked: "Wasn't it possible that the man was done away with at home?" Later that day, he tried the conjure ball again, and he said the body had been found.

Alfred says it was an old man named Jack Collis who told them they should look around the house. (And Collis or Chollis was a witness at the trial.) He poked around the ashes in the fireplace with his walking cane and said, "There's too many bits of bone in this fireplace and the ashes are too greasy. They found more bits of bone in fresh ashes that had been poured into a "mortar hole" near the spring. Alfred says this was where they found a heel iron like the kind Charlie wore on his hunting moccasins. (Henry Spainhour wrote that a blacksmith testified at the trial that the heel iron was one he'd made for Charles Silver.) Under the floorboards, they found "a circle of blood as large as a hog's liver." Alfred did not mention it, but Charles' skull must also have been found because the indictment describes the wound to his head in detail.

Again, much of this was printed in the Rutherfordton newspaper 70 years before Alfred Silver gave his version of what happened. "At length, some one in examining the fire-place, discovered human bones, nearly consumed, in the ashes! The search within and around the house was renewed. A portion of the body, partly consumed by fire, was found buried a short distance from the house — large puddles of blood were also discovered beneath the floor of the house and in a bench was a deep gash made with an axe, together with blood, where to appearance the head of the victim had been chopped off. It is said that the neighbors residing two or three miles distant perceived a very strange and offensive odour in the air, at the time the body is supposed to have been burning."

The State v. Frankie Silver

With all this "strong and convincing evidence," Alfred Silver said, a jury was summoned and an inquest held. He does not say where the inquest was held but since the members whose names we know were close neighbors, it is likely they visited the scene of the crime itself. The jury of inquest found probable cause and ordered the arrest of Frankie Silver, Barbary Stuard and Blackston Stuard. (The name "Joseph Stuard" was crossed out in this and one other document.) The three were taken to jail in Morganton the next day, January 10, 1832.

Isaiah Stewart may have been a poor uneducated man, but he swung into action in ferocious defense of his family. He was able to get two justices of the peace to order a habeas corpus hearing because he said his wife, daughter and son had been committed to jail "without the legal forms of trial" and "without...having it in their power to confront their accusers before any legal tribunal." A later document says the father "believes the defendants were committed on the verdict of the Jury of Inquest alone, and without the form of trial as required by law."

Frankie herself was bound over for trial and held in jail, but her mother and brother were released on January 17, 1832, because "there appearing no evidence on behalf of the state against them." They were, however, ordered to appear in court in Morganton on the fourth Monday of March "to give evidence on behalf of the state against Francy Silvers...." Isaiah Stuart was ordered to post a bond of 100 pounds to ensure that his wife and son would appear at the trial.

44

Morganton 1832

The wonderfully eccentric naturalist and journalist Silas McDowell has left us a contemporary description of Morganton at this time.

Born May 16, 1795, in York District, S.C., McDowell was the son of Elizabeth and the grandson of Pacolet William McDowell, a cousin of the distinguished Burke County family of that name. He arrived in Morganton in 1816, at the age of 21, after learning the tailor's trade in Charleston.

As a young man, McDowell was the guide for a number of famous botanists who came to explore the uncharted regions of western North Carolina. The English botanist, John Lyons, quite literally died in his arms at the Eagle Hotel in Asheville.

McDowell eventually settled on a farm near Franklin in Macon County, where he died in 1879. In his last years, he dictated several lengthy memoirs about his life to his daughter. His years in Morganton are described in an unpublished manuscript, "Morganton and Its Surroundings Sixty Years Ago," a typed copy of which is in the Southern Historical Collection at UNC-Chapel Hill.

The town, he said, consisted of "a shabby, weatherbeaten courthouse, a frame, weatherboarded structure without paint; and a jail in keeping with it, a mere weatherboarded pen, built of hewed logs with a door and two windows like portholes, and secured with iron bars. But, as an offset there was hardby a splendid two story whipping post and pillory. The public grounds covered two acres and facing this was the McEntire hotel, Walton's store opposite, and then David Tate's dwelling, a rambling frame building long and lonesome, suggestive of rats. Tate was west of the public buildings. John Caldwells house was north, a white painted house on the corner and the only clean looking house on the outside in the place. The only other house on that side not built of logs was a low frame building in which Col. W.W. Erwin kept a bank and his son, James Avery, a store. The next house east was the residence of an old German and his lady, (no children), his name was John H. Stevely. His house looked like a barn, weatherboarded, but unstained by paint. These were all the buildings facing the public ground. The back buildings were these: Dr. Bouchell's and Major John M'Guires. These buildings had some claim to architectural taste. And there was no other house in 1816, save the one down the Hunting Creek Road, a fourth mile from the courthouse."

McDowell concluded that "Morganton, as a seat of justice for the large and wealthy county of Burke is decidedly a shabby town; while Morganton's location as a standpoint to look over the most magnificent valley in the world is the most interesting spot I ever beheld." He spoke with familiarity of the high mountains — Grandfather, the Roan, Yellow and Black Mountains — because he'd been on the tops of every one.

There was no church in the whole town when McDowell arrived. However, he wrote that the town began to change within a year. It was then that the first Presbyterian church was built, along with male and female academies and several nice brick houses.

A new jail was completed in 1826, he records, but the commissioners refused to accept it because it was built of bad brick. The brick jail must have been in use by the time Frankie was brought there because she was known to have been kept in the "dungeon" and it's not likely that a log pen would have had a dungeon.

A new courthouse was also under construction, although it would not be completed until 1835 and would not be occupied until 1838. Frankie's jailer or "Gaoler" as he spelled it, John Maguire, would be put in charge of the new building, which still stands, serving now as a county museum.

The Grand Jury Indictment

Apparently the grand jury did not indict Frankie Silver until the opening of the spring term of superior court, the fourth Monday of March, 1832, since "spring term" is the only date appearing on the document. (A copy of the indictment and all other documents referred to in Part Two appear in Part Four.)

The indictment — which follows an archaic form that stretches one sentence through more than 500 words — charged that Frances Silver, Blackston Stuart and Barbara Stuart "not having the fear of God before their eyes, but being moved and seduced by the instigation of the Devil on the twenty second day of December in the year of our Lord one thousand eight hundred and thirty one, with force and arms in the county of Burke aforesaid in and upon one Charles Silver in the peace of God and of the State then and there being feloniously willfully and of true malice aforethought did make an assault...."

It charges that Frankie held an axe valued at six pence in both hands and gave Charlie a mortal wound in the head three inches long and an inch deep, killing him instantly. It went on to charge Frankie's mother and brother with "aiding, helping, abetting, assisting, comforting and maintaining the said Frances Silver in the felony of murder...."

The members of the grand jury who delivered the indictment were: Samuel C. Tate, foreman, Archibald Berry, William Wakefield, William Coffey, Joseph Scott, William Wacker, Ruckets Stanly, James Bergin, Bryant Gibbs, James McCall, William Gragg, David Glass, William I. Tate, Thomas Morrison, Isaac Hicks, George Corpening, George Holloway, and Jesse Richardson Hyatt.

Witnesses for the state included Charles' father, Jacob, his sister, Margaret, and uncles, Thomas and John Silver. Other state witnesses were Nancy Wilson, John Collis, Joseph Tate, Thomas Howell, William Hutchins and D.D. Baker.

The grand jury returned a true bill of indictment only against Frankie Silver and all charges were thus dismissed against her mother and brother.

Other witnesses subpoenaed for the coming trial for the state included Charles' uncle, Green (Greenberry) Silver, Nelly Silver, Thomas Howell, William Hutchins, Jacob Hutchins, Elijah Green, and Joseph Tate. Curiously, Alfred Silver was not subpoenaed, maybe because he was under age.

Only three witnesses were subpoenaed to testify for Frankie: Isaac Grindstaff, Jacob Hutchins, and William Hutchins. In one of the later petitions, Isaac Grindstaff identifies himself as a member of the inquest jury; it could be that Jacob and William Hutchins were also called to testify about the inquest.

Justice was indeed swift in those days and apparently Frankie Silver was immediately brought in for arraignment after the indictment was read in open court. She pleaded not guilty and the following jury was promptly called "to pass upon the life and death of the Prisoner at the bar, Frances Silver": Henry Pain, Robert McElrath, David Beedle, Oscar Willis, Cyrus P. Connelly, John Hall, William L. Baird, Richard Bean, Joseph Tipps, Lafayette Collins, Robert Garrison, David Hunsaker.

The Members of the Court

The trial of Frankie Silver brought together some of the best legal minds in the state at that time. The superior court judge was John Robert Donnell, who had traveled to the mountain circuit from his home in New Bern; the prosecutor was William Julius Alexander; Frankie's defense lawyer was Thomas Worth Wilson; and the very young clerk of court was Burgess Sidney Gaither.

The judge's surname has been frequently misspelled as "Daniel" over the years. I think the reason for that is obvious. Daniel was a common name in the area, Donnell was not. Born in Scotland in 1789, John Robert Donnell was graduated with honors from the University of North Carolina in 1807. He married Margaret Elizabeth Spaight, daughter of Gov. Richard Dobbs Spaight, in 1816. Their son, Richard Spaight Donnell was a state senator, speaker of the North Carolina House of Commons and a U.S. congressman.

Judge Donnell was described by a contemporary as a typical Scot, "a rigid economist" who skillfully managed the properties he inherited from an uncle and his wife's family until they were worth more than $500,000 at that time, a multi-million-dollar fortune by today's standards. His wife died at 31 in 1831 and he never remarried.

Stephen F. Miller described him in *Newbern Fifty Years Ago* as "a quiet, unobtrusive, upright gentleman, and used to bear with quiet equanimity the biting sarcasm which Mr. [John] Stanly was in the habit of thrusting at the court whenever it suited his policy."

When Union forces took over New Bern during the Civil War, Donnell took refuge in Raleigh, where he died in 1864.

In 1942, a number of Donnell's personal papers were found in a safe deposit box when a Raleigh bank closed. These were turned over to the Southern Historical Collection at Chapel Hill, but unfortunately there is no mention of the Frankie Silver case in any of them — nor in any other papers relating to Donnell that I could find. Neither is the case mentioned in any of the several biographical sketches published about Donnell in various North Carolina history texts.

Frankie's prosecutor, William Julius Alexander, was born at Salisbury in March of 1797. He graduated at the University of North Carolina in 1816 and after serving an apprenticeship under Archibald Henderson, was admitted to the bar in 1818. He married Catharine Wilson, daughter of "the great solicitor," Joseph Wilson. Wilson was born in 1780, the son of William Wilson, who came from Scotland to Edenton in 1720, and of Eunice Worth, whose family came from Nantucket Island to join a Quaker community in what is now Greensboro.

Joseph Wilson was the great, great grandfather of the late Sen. Sam J. Ervin Jr., and Ervin has written with admiraton of his ancestor: "After attending David Caldwell's school in Greensboro and Greeneville College in Greeneville, Tenn., Joseph studied law under Reuben Wood, an energetic, erudite lawyer and public servant who traveled on horseback carrying Bacon's Maximims of the law and Blackstone's Commentaries on the Laws of England in his saddlebags to virtually all courts sitting in the vast area lying between his home in Randolph County and Jonesboro, Tenn."

Joseph Wilson would marry the daughter of his mentor Reuben Wood and they moved to Charlotte in 1812 after he was named solicitor for the Sixth Judicial Circuit, known as the mountain circuit because it included all of the counties from Mecklenburg to the Tennessee border.

It was a time of high crime in what was still the frontier of North Carolina and Wilson was an agressive prosecutor, so aggressive his life was threatened several times. In his will, he wrote that he expected to be murdered. In fact, he apparently died of natural causes at home in Charlotte on August 27, 1829, although he was only 49 years old at the time.

The General Assembly named Wilson's son-in-law, William J. Alexander, to replace him as solicitor for the Sixth Circuit. In Joseph Wilson's will, his executors are listed as his son-in-law and his younger brother, Thomas Worth Wilson, who in March of 1832 would square off as legal adversaries in the trial of Frances Stuart Silver.

From the time he was in college, Sam Ervin was a prolific writer of articles and essays, not just about legal questions but also about local and family history. He was fascinated by the Frankie Silver case and wrote several articles about it. Unfortunately, he had accepted Kemp Battle's word that Frankie's lawyer was Nicholas Woodfin, and Ervin never knew that her lawyer (whom he soundly criticized for his handling of the case) was his own great, great, great uncle, although he wrote a short biography of the man.

According to Ervin's account in the Heritage of Burke County, Thomas Worth Wilson was born March 7, 1792. He first practiced law in Wilkesboro and represented Wilkes County in the North Carolina House of Commons from 1824-1826. He moved to Morganton in 1830 and established a very successful farm on the old Morganton-Salem road. When his younger brother, Jethro Wilson, a widower, died in November of 1836 in Tennessee, Thomas Wilson took in two of the orphans and raised them on his farm along with his own children, Mary Jane, who was born in 1831, Joseph, who was born in 1833, and Ruth Elizabeth, or Betty Wilson, who was born in 1840.

The 1850 census lists Wilson as the owner of 25 slaves. However, he was already in financial trouble by that time, having left a client named Daniel Angel quite literally to hang in Yancey County in 1847. Angel's family appealed to another lawyer, saying the condemned man was forced to go into court "without his witnesses or any atterny, on the a count of said Willson removing...he has haponed to some missfortons and has left the country...." Thomas Worth Wilson moved to Seguin, Guadalupe County, Texas, and died there October 17, 1863, a string of debtors' notices in the justice of the peace courts his only legacy.

The Trial and Legal Questions

Little is known about Frankie's trial, except that it was concluded in less than two days. In the documents that accompanied the appeal to the North Carolina Supreme Court, we learn: "The case was taken up for trial on Thursday morning and occupied the day in the examining of testimony, the argument of council and the charge of the court. The Jury having retired from the Bar under the charge of officers about candle light. The jury were kept together in deliberations during the night and on the next day returned to the Bar and was called over they stated that they had not yet agreed and expressed a wish to hear some of the witnesses who had been examined again brought into Court that they might be satisfied about their testimony."

Other details come from one of the first petitions to the governor after Frankie's conviction: "We are cognizant of the fact that she was convicted on Circumstantial evidence alone and that after hearing the evidence as given out of Counsel & charge of the Judge the Jury retired and returned into court nine for acquitting & three for convicting but owing to the re-examination of witnesses in behalf of the state running into a Trane of Circumstances that were not related in the former examination and which the prisoner had not the opportunity of explaining as she had not introduced any testimony on the first examination. She was precluded by the rule adopted by the court — that no new witness should be examined at that stage of the trial nor remarks of counsel heard...."

From all our sources, we know only that the prosecutor introduced as evidence that a heel iron found in the ashes at Frankie's cabin belonged to Charlie and that Charlie was supposed to have been asleep when he was attacked. However, we know next to nothing about what Thomas Wilson said in Frankie's defense. This is extraordinary because there are three very long letters from Wilson to Governors Stokes and Swain about the case. Even as the counselor is pleading for the woman's life, his language is so vague as to be almost incomprehensible.

Wilson wrote Gov. Swain on June 3, 1833, and reviewed the case this way: "The evidence against your petitioner was entirely circumstantial — NO one knows but your petitioner the circumstances and the truth of the facts under which the act was committed — Being a woman and entirely ignorant of the laws of the country she felt a repugnance to making any confession from a fear of involving herself in still greater difficulties."

In another letter to Swain, dated June 12, 1833, Wilson said "it was clearly a case of manslaughter if not Justifiable Homicide. This was always my opinion from the Circumstances Proved and the facts attending the case. I am confident if the facts could have been proved as they really were that it would have amounted to no more than manslaughter...."

You have to ask at this point: If her lawyer felt so strongly, why wasn't he able to prove his case in court?

The legal questions involved are both simple and complex.

Some have speculated that Frankie was not allowed to take the stand because of her sex. However, even though women had very few rights at that time, they could testify in court. Several of the witnesses against Frankie were women.

The point of law involved the evidentiary rules of the English common law which was still in force in North Carolina at that time. Under these, the accused was deemed an incompetent witness and could not take the stand in his or her own defense. Although the criminal code was revised in 1835 when North Carolina adopted a new constitution, it was not until 1857 when the old common law rule was rejected in favor of laws that said the accused could testify but could not be compelled to testify against his or her will.

Even if Frankie was barred from testifying, however, her lawyer most assuredly could have presented a case of self defense. In hindsight, this, of course, would have been the more reasonable course.

Thomas Wilson, surely in consultation with Frankie's persistent father, obviously felt the best course was to deny everything. He would let the state try to prove Frankie did it and then try to knock down the state's circumstantial case. (Of course, very few murders take place before witnesses and a "chain of circumstances" is the most common method of proving a murderer guilty.) Here, Frankie's lawyer miscalculated and lost the case.

We have this on the authority of an eye-witness to the trial, Burgess Sidney Gaither.

Born in Iredell County on March 16, 1807, Gaither was only 22 years old when he was admitted to the bar in North Carolina. He moved to Morganton that same year, 1829, and a year later, he was named clerk of court. He would go on to enjoy a distinguished career as lawyer, solicitor, speaker of the North Carolina Senate, a member of the Confederate congress and superintendent of the U.S. Mint. He would live to the age of almost 85, dying on February 23, 1892, one of Morganton's most revered gentlemen of the bar.

Although I have never been able to find anything Gaither wrote about Frankie Silver's guilt or innocence, the fact remains that as clerk, he was in court every minute of the trial and he personally transcribed nearly all of the documents relating to the case. And his was the very first signature on the first petition asking the governor to pardon Frankie for her crime. He believed she should not be hanged from the very beginning, in other words, and apparently expressed this opinion until his dying days.

Gaither had been a very close friend of Sam Ervin Sr. and had talked with him in some detail about the case, all of which was passed on to Ervin's son when he came along and showed a strong interest in history and the law. In an article published in the *Morganton News-Herald* April 3, 1924, Sam Ervin Jr. wrote: "The late Colonel B.S. Gaither, who was the youthful clerk of the Superior Court at the time of her trial and execution and who witnessed a remarkable retentive memory, was wont to asssert that she would not have been convicted if the truth had been disclosed on the trial.

"According to Colonel Gaither, Silver mistreated his wife and she killed him in protection of herself. And Colonel Gaither always entertained the opinion that if the defense had admitted the killing the jury would have found her act justified and would have acquitted her. The defense, however, was a denial that the hand of Frankie Silver struck the fatal blow and there being evidence of her guilt, the jury following the instinct of the sleuth which lurks in every human mind, promptly convicted her of wilful murder."

According to the surviving documents, the jurors were given the case on a Thursday. They debated that entire night and came back the next morning with questions for certain witnesses. One source says they had already voted nine to three for acquittal at this time, but they were obviously satisfied with the new evidence presented by the witnesses and came back with a unanimous verdict of guilty.

One document tells us that the verdict and sentencing did not take place that Friday, but on the following Monday, which would have been April 2, 1832. Frankie was sentenced to be hanged by the neck until dead on the following July 27. However, her lawyer succeeded in getting an appeal to the North Carolina Supreme Court. (Under our current laws, all capital cases are automatically reviewed by the state supreme court.)

Several lawyers examining the records recently told me they were appalled to find that Frankie's lawyer's name does not appear anywhere in the appeal documents. The reason is quite simple.

At that time, the judge himself not only decided whether there would be an appeal or not, he decided which points would justify the appeal — and actually wrote the appeal himself.

As Judge Donnell phrased it, the appeal was based solely on the fact that the witnesses, who had been sequestered before their testimony, had been dismissed and allowed to mingle and confer before they were called back for new questioning by the jury.

In his convoluted way, Frankie's lawyer would complain to the governor that it wasn't just the mingling of witnesses but the fact that new testimony was presented and the defense had no chance to cross-examine or rebut the new evidence with new witnesses. (When the witnesses were brought back, the jurors could ask questions, but the lawyers could not.)

At least, that's what I think he was trying to say in the following: "I have never been satisfied with the case made for the Supreme Court by his honor Judge Donnell. The witness[es] after the Jury had retired & had been out for the space of twenty four hours were permitted (by the court) to under go a re-examination by the jury and that too on the very subject & ground taken for her defense & which before had not been touched by them. I still believe that if the case had been fairly presented to the Supreme Court that she must have had the advantage of a new trial."

Appeal to the Supreme Court

There were no oral arguments before the Supreme Court in Frankie's case. The justices had only the documents passed along from the lower court in Morganton: the indictment, the judge's own summary of the trial and the defense lawyer's objections regarding the separation of witnesses.

In his summary, Donnell noted that at the request of the jurors he had ordered that certain witnesses be returned to answer questions during the jury's deliberations.

"The Jurors asked the questions and on some points the witnesses went more into detail than they had done on their first examination. The Prisoner's Counsel remarked that the witnesses had been separated during the trial but had come to the bar and had been at large during the night and the court stated to the jury that such was the case that it could not have been anticipated that they would wish to hear any of the witnesses examined again after the case had been put to them and they had returned from the Bar. But that the Jury ought to hear the witnesses with all the prejudice arising from the circumstances of their having had an opportunity of being together since their former examination.

"The jury returned a verdict of guilty. The Prisoner's counsel obtained a rule to show cause why a new trial should not be granted on the ground that the witnesses had been permitted to be examined by the jury on the second day when the witnesses had had an opportunity of being together after their first examination. Rule discharged and Judgment of Death. Appealed to the Supreme Court."

Justice Thomas Ruffin's language was clear as a bell compared to that of everybody else involved in this case.

He wrote in his opinion for the court: "The separation of witnesses is adopted in aid of the cross-examination, as a test of the truth of their testimony by its consistency or inconsistency. It is not founded on the idea of keeping the witnesses from intercourse with each other. That would be a vain attempt. The expectation is not to prevent the fabrication of false stories, but by separate cross-examinations to detect them."

Ruffin also pointed out that it was not unusual for witnesses to be kept together in the same room once they'd testified, even though they knew they could be called back for additional testimony by either side.

If there had been any attempt to introduce incompetent evidence, Ruffin said, the court would surely have interdicted it. "But here the reexamination was solely to satisfy the jury of the testimony already given, and the greater detail made necessary only to produce that satisfaction. So we must consider it, for the objection is not taken to the subjects of the interrogatories, or the nature of the answers, but only that the witnesses were examined at all after having been together. In that I see nothing against either practice or principle. *Per Curiam.* The Judgement Be Affirmed. Thomas Ruffin."

The following notice was sent back to the court in Morganton, and it remains on file in the clerk of court's office there along with other documents relating to The State of North Carolina v. Frances Silver: "It is considered by the court that the judgment of the Superior Court of Law for the county of Burke be affirmed. And it is ordered that the said Superior Court proceed to judgment and sentence of death against the defendant Frances Silver. On motion judgment is granted against Jackson Stuart and Isaiah Stuart, sureties to the appeal, for the costs of this court in this suit incurred. Certified by Jno. L. Henderson, Clk."

The sentencing was set for the fall term of Burke Superior Court, with Judge David Lowry Swain presiding. But not long before the court was to convene, Swain was seriously injured in a carriage accident. The fall session of court was canceled and all business was put off until the spring term.

In a letter dated September 16, 1832, W.R. Lenoir wrote: "In consequence of the misfortune of Judge Swain falling from his sulky when on his way to meet his circuit, we will have no court this week — he rec'd considerable injury. One of his arms fractured, and a shoulder dislocated & sustained bruises elsewhere."

In December of 1832, Swain gave up his judgeship after he was elected governor by the General Assembly to replace Gov. Montfort Stokes, who had been appointed Commissioner of Indian Affairs and moved to the Indian Territory and what would become Oklahoma.

The Efforts to Save Frankie from the Gallows

In light of current politics, it would be fascinating to know that spousal abuse entered into the defense of Frances Silver in 1832. In one of the later petitions to the governor, there are the intriguing words that Charles' abuse of Frankie was "in evidence."

However, that surely meant only that people knew about his treatment of her, not that it was an issue in the trial. It could have been introduced as evidence, of course, if her lawyer had pleaded self defense. However, it's difficult to imagine the lawyer's introducing extenuating circumstances when he's saying she did not commit the murder.

Although it was an extremely difficult thing to prove in those male-dominated times, spousal abuse or cruelty was recognized by the state and by the courts as grounds for divorce and so presumably might also have offered a defense for justifiable homicide. Under the legislative act of 1814, amending the original divorce laws of 1808, cruelty was recognized as a legitimate cause for divorce. Until 1827, the General Assembly had to give final approval on all divorces in the state; after that, divorces were handled by the superior courts. Of the 266 petitions for divorce prior to 1827, only 11 cited cruelty as the cause; it ranked number seven in the list of causes for divorce.

However, if Charles' abuse of Frankie was never introduced as evidence in the trial, it was without question the reason public opinion suddenly shifted in Frankie' s favor after the trial. The public had first been swayed by reports of how Frankie had disposed of the body, but the very natural sympathy for a female who was also a young mother began to turn in Frankie's favor the longer she stayed in jail and people began to think again about her plight and to hear that her husband had frequently beaten her.

Also, it is a fact that her sex played a key role in the sympathies that were aroused to try and save her. Sexist though it may seem in light of current attitudes, it cannot be denied that there has always been an enormous gender inequity in the history of capital punishment in North Carolina and America.

In the 17 different letters and petitions sent to the governor to get a pardon for Frankie Silver, it is a recurring theme from the first to last that this is too harsh a punishment for a woman, especially a woman who has been abused by her husband and may have killed him in self defense.

It is not a question of sexism but of humanity to those of us who feel strongly that killing another human being is wrong whether it is carried out by the state or by an individual. While there is no evidence that the death penalty has ever served as a deterrent to crime in America, there is ample evidence that the state itself has set an example that violence, murder, is some sort of solution to crime. The pity is not that we feel more compassion for women than men on death row, but that we don't have the same compassion for men waiting to be killed by the state.

The 17 letters and petitions to Governors Montfort Stokes and David Lowry Swain contradict a hundred different details in the story of Frankie Silver as it was handed down and embellished over the years by ballad singers and writers for newspapers and magazines. As far as I can determine, I was the first person to find these papers in the North Carolina archives in September of 1963 and the first to make use of them in articles I wrote about the case. I came upon them by a circuitous route. When I was a junior in high school, I wrote two term papers, one on the murder of Charles Silver and the other on Nicholas Washington Woodfin, the lawyer and plantation owner who gave his name to the community just north of Asheville where I was born.

Like a hundred others before me, I accepted the misstatement of fact that Woodfin had been Frankie Silver's lawyer. In researching my little paper, I visited Woodfin's granddaughter, Eliza Woodfin Holland Underwood, and her nephew, John Woodfin Holland, the last surviving relatives of this once rich and famous man. Jack, the nephew (whose father had been a reporter for the New York Herald) had degenerated into alcoholism and made a pitiful living as a delivery boy for the Pack Square Pharmacy in Asheville.

Eliza had been poet laureate of the United Confederate Veterans and while still a young woman had fortunately married one of the old veterans — because a pittance of a widow's pension was all she had to live on in her last years. She and her nephew lived in two dingy rooms in an old house near downtown Asheville. Eliza wrote in her diary one typical day that they had only a can of tuna fish and a bowl of cornflakes left to eat. But out their back window, they could still see the fine old Greek Revival mansion built by her grandfather. It stood at the corner of Woodfin Street and Broadway in downtown Asheville until it was torn down in the 1960s for a hideously garish new building for the Clyde Savings and Loan Company.

Moving from one cheap rooming house to another, Eliza had made sure she always had a view of the old mansion. "It is my anchor," she wrote. It was all she had to hold onto of the grandeur that had once been her family's. Through my senior year in high school, I would go by to visit with Miss Eliza. She described me as a choir boy with the face of an angel, which doubtless tells more about her destitute loneliness than about my appearance at that time. She was thrilled that I was interested in history, especially her family history.

The nephew died first and then dear old Eliza when I was a freshman at UNC in 1960. There were no heirs, and only a few very old friends attended her funeral. My mother got a call from Eliza's landlady. She was trying to clean out the rooms Eliza had rented and there were all these old papers. She asked if I wanted to go through them before she threw them all out. I went by and carted away box after box of clippings and old letters and documents. I gave the McDowell and Woodfin family Bibles to the library in Asheville; the other old papers I assembled and took in to Dr. James Patton, who was then director of the Southern Historical Collection at UNC-Chapel Hill.

Patton was delighted that a teenager had taken such an interest in history and in helping to save a fairly important number of McDowell and Woodfin family papers. I asked if he'd ever heard of Nicholas Woodfin and he gave a wry smile, shifted his pipe, and gestured toward a very fine oil portrait hanging behind his desk. "That's him," he said.

Nobody had any idea how the portrait of a young Nicholas Woodfin had ended up at UNC, but there it was. (It now hangs in the SHC's research room.) Woodfin had not attended the university, but he had served as the university's lawyer and escheator in western North Carolina during the long period when his friend and mentor, David L. Swain was president.

There were a dozen different biographical sketches of Woodfin in the various histories of North Carolina. He had represented the state in the infamous Littlefield-Swepson case, in which two carpetbaggers made off with millions of state railroad funds. He had been involved in many other famous cases, but nowhere did I find any mention of the Frankie Silver case.

Working with Dr. Patton and the extraordinary collection of manuscripts in the SHC, I was then led to the North Carolina Archives in Raleigh. Since Woodfin had been a close friend and partner of David Lowry Swain, I figured there might be some letters he had written to Swain when he was governor about his defense of Frankie Silver. In September of 1963, I sat in the search room of the archives, poring over the letters and petitions to Governors Stokes and Swain — and the details of the Frankie Silver story as I had heard it and read about it were shattered in my mind forever.

Here was proof positive that she was neither the first nor only white woman ever hanged in North Carolina. Her lawyer was not Woodfin, but a man named Thomas Worth Wilson. Hundreds of people had believed she should never have been hanged and had tried to save her from the gallows. This was not the "Frankie and Johnny" tale of jealousy and revenge I'd been raised to believe in. I was mortified that a poor woman had been so wrongly defamed by generations of storytellers, ballad singers and, worst, my own kind, local historians and writers for newspapers and magazines.

In 1973, at the height of the Watergate hearings, I wrote to Sen. Sam Ervin Jr., who was chairman of that historic committee whose work would lead to the resignation of President Richard Nixon. In spite of the weight of current history on his shoulders, Sen. Ervin took time out to write me about the unjust fate of Frankie Silver 140 years earlier. He had been born and lived his whole life just a few blocks from the spot where she was hanged in old Morganton.

"Like you," he said in a letter to me, "I believe that tradition has done her a grave injustice."

The change in public opinion in favor of Frankie is documented in the very first letter to Gov. Montfort Stokes, dated September 6, 1832. Colonel David Newland writes in reference to a meeting he had with the governor at his home in Wilkesboro in April, just days after Frankie's conviction. At that time, Newland says the governor wanted to know if a woman had ever been hanged in North Carolina and Newland said he didn't think so. Newland also wrote that he had then felt "if rumors be trew I thought her a fit subject for example."

In other words, she should be punished for her crime. However, he had since had a change of heart, "from various information which I have rec'd since her trial I am induced to believe her gilt [sic] has been much exaggerated which you will perceive by the opinion some gentlemen of the Bar who has assigned her petition & was present & also disinterested during her trial. Upon the whole I realy think her a fit subject for executive Clemency."

Born March 12, 1762, in Lunenburg County, Virginia, Montfort Stokes had gone to sea at an early age and joined the Continental Navy as soon as the Revolutionary War broke out. Captured by the British, he spent several months as a prisoner in New York. After the war, he read law at his older brother John's office in Salisbury and then went on to a long career of public service. (John Stokes, for whom Stokes County was named, would become North Carolina's first federal judge.) Montfort Stokes served as clerk of the N.C. Senate for 18 years and was elected by the General Assembly to serve as a U.S. Senator from 1816 to 1823. He was elected governor by the Assembly in 1831 and re-elected in 1832, resigning on December 6, 1832 when he was named Commissioner of Indian Affairs by President Andrew Jackson.

This position required that he move to Fort Gibson in what is now Oklahoma and that is where he died on November 4, 1842. Stokes' second wife was Rachel, daughter of Hugh Montgomery, who was the Royal officer in charge of putting down the Regulators in Hillsborough. They had five sons and five daughters. Their son, Hugh Montgomery Stokes, was a young lawyer following the circuit courts who would become involved in the cause of Frankie Silver.

Montfort Stokes is described in William S. Powell's *Dictionary of North Carolina Biography* as "an inveterate politician, but his love of gambling and his dangerous temper frequently got him into trouble. He was once wounded in a duel with Jesse A. Pearson of Rowan."

What I discovered in reading through the hundreds of papers in the governor's official documents and private correspondence was that 80 to 90 percent of those papers involved letters and petitions from people trying to get pardons for people convicted of capital crimes. In almost every case, Governor Stokes granted those pardons.

On June 8, 1832, he issued the following declaration: "Whereas it has been made known to me by the petition of many respectable citizens of the county of Mecklenburg in the State of North Carolina: by the representation of several gentlemen of the Bar, and by a copy of record in the case, that at the last Superior Court of law held for the said county of Mecklenburg, a certain Sally Barnicastle was convicted of the crime of Infanticide and sentenced to be hanged on the 30th instant. It further appears that the testimony in the case was altogether circumstantial; and although sufficient to satisfy the jury of her guilt, yet they were induced to record as part of the verdict 'that they think it a case in which she is entitled to Executive clemency.' And whereas a number of respectable persons, including the examining Physicians and one of the prosecuting attorneys, have represented the Prisoner as a proper object for the exercise of Executive clemency: Now therefore know ye, that for this and other causes, and in pursuance of the power vested in me by the Constitution of the said State of North Carolina, I do hereby pardon the said Sally Barnicastle for the crime aforesaid: Of which the Sheriff of Mecklenburg County and all others concerned are required to take notice and govern themselves accordingly...."

Although the two petitions on behalf of Frankie Silver addressed to Gov. Stokes bear no dates, they were apparently written and signed during the summer of 1832 after the state supreme court had rejected Frankie's appeal and ordered the lower court to set a new date to carry out its death sentence. One petition was signed by 113 men, a second by 40. The first signatures are of lawyers in Morganton, starting with Burgess Gaither, David Newland and Frankie's own lawyer, Thomas Wilson. But, interesting enough, the signatories to the second petition include the names of several of the close neighbors of the Silver and Stewart families — the families of Hoppes, McNeill, Howell, and Ainsworth.

Without meaning to impugn the motives of the jury, the first petitioners gave the following reasons for saying Frankie deserved to be pardoned: "That the Verdict was founded entirely on circumstantial evidence there is no doubt. That the defendant is young, not exceeding the years of 20 or 22 even now, was raised most of the life right in the county of Burke of Low and humble parentage who have ever been incapable of administering either to the mind or body — such comfort as Nature and Childhood may have required. They represent that the defendant has now an infant child which has been refused her sight ever since she has been immured within the walls of a dungeon which took place the first of January last, the alleged time of the Committing of the offense. They further represent that the defendant has suffered greatly in health since her confinement and is now laboring under disease as they are informed and believe. Your petitioners further represent to your excellency that they represent to your excellency that the execution of a poor woman whose very name tis frailty for example's sake is not called for by the Publick or for the good of County. The only inducement on the part of the defendant for the Commission of the alleged offense was that of brutal conduct of the husband toward the wife — as appeared in evidence. Your petitioners do further represent to your excellency that the execution of a poor female for an alleged offense of this character has so seldom occurred within the history of our county whilst it has so frequently happened that husbands have murdered their wives and escaped Punishment that we believe it would reflect indictable disgrace on the Community."

The second petition begins with the curious observation that "there is so much doubt" about the crime "as the body has never been found." It goes on to say that the petitioners don't believe a woman could have committed such a crime. "We the undersigned believe that the circumstances which are supposed to have attended this murder are so totally inconsistent with human nature that the greatest exertion of female fortitude could not possible have accomplished the horrid deed. We are many of us the neighbors of the prisoner and know her to be a woman of good character and have never heard her charged with any offense heretofore."

After his letter to Stokes on September 6, Newland visited the governor in Raleigh. He wrote to Stokes on September 22: "On my return from Raleigh I was anxiously hailed believing I had obtained from your excellency a pardon for Francis Silvers. On reporting that you had not yet determined whether you would pardon her or not it seemed to strike some of your friends with considerable surprise."

Newland also said he had just learned that the signers of the petitions he had delivered to the governor included seven of the 12 jurors who had convicted Frankie. However, it is clear from the letter that the governor had told Newland to tell Frankie's lawyer, Thomas Wilson, he would need the signatures of all 12 jurors in order to get a pardon.

Wilson assured Newland he would do this, but it's obvious he was never able to get all 12 jurors to sign a petition. Newland concluded his letter to Stokes: "But whither he does or not from this additional fact before you (that seven of the 12 had already asked for a pardon) I cannot help but believe your good hospitable and friendly feelings together with your good judgment will extend mercy to an humbe & penitent Convict."

On October 29, 1832, Hugh Montgomery Stokes wrote his father from the family estate in Wilkesboro, that Frankie Silver's father, Isaiah Stewart, had been to visit asking if the governor had or was going to pardon Frankie. The son says that court officials in Morganton were complaining about the cost of keeping a prisoner for such a long time. This, Hugh Stokes wryly observes, is "a very common complaint to hide the operation of the laws."

The younger Stokes refers to an earlier letter in which he had set forth all the facts surrounding the case, but unfortunately that letter is missing from the governor's papers and letterbooks. In the second letter, he says he has just been to Burke County and "the excitement against the culprit is rapidly subsiding: and I have but little hesitation in saying it will totally subside before the re-condemnation [that is, the second sentencing to death] can be made except with the family and connections of the husband of Mrs. Silvers...."

Governor Stokes must have been still concerned about whether a woman had ever been hanged in North Carolina because the son wrote him: "I know of but one execution of a white woman since the formation of our present government, though there may have been more." He concludes his letter by urging his father to show mercy "toward the weaker part of creation" and grant a pardon to Frankie Silver.

With this letter, Hugh Montgomery Stokes disappears from the history books. I could find no further mention of him anywhere except for a memoir of the legal profession published in a Morganton newspaper in the late 19th century.

Whiskey was a problem for the lawyers as well as their clients in those days. Riding to court one day and desperate for a drink, an older lawyer spied a bulge in a younger lawyer's saddlebags. He asked the younger one to produce the whiskey and was told the bulge was caused by lawbooks. Whereupon the older one said: "You'll never make a lawyer till you learn to carry your law in your head and liquor in your saddlebags." Hugh Stokes, the memoirist continues, "yielded to the same weakness and made his life a sad failure."

Although his was among the first signatures on the first petition, Frankie's lawyer did not write to the governor until November 19, 1832. By that time Gov. Stokes must have known he would soon be appointed Indian Commissioner because he would resign less than a month later to take the new post.

Thomas Wilson, of course, had no way of knowing this and wrote with great feeling for "the unfortunate Lady who is now confined in our jail in Morganton Franky Silvers. She has been induced for some time to believe a pardon had been granted by your excellency. This opinion got abroad through a misunderstanding of Col. David Newland. It is not necessary that I should multiply words or reasons why I think she should win a pardon. Suffer it to say that I have no hesitation in saying that the community expect her a pardon & I believe generally wish it."

Wilson went on to say that "There certainly are but few now who think or wish her execution. It is believed by many that her parents were very instrumental in the perpetration of that horrid deed. If so, surely it is a powerful reason why the executive clemency should be extended to one of her age and condtion."

And then Wilson says something that may explain why Gov. Stokes was so reluctant to exercise another pardon: "I know my dear sir that you have often been reproached for extending the Pardon's Power...." But, he continues, "You have nothing to fear in this reproach. Humanity is certainly one of the greatest attributes. I do hope and trust Sir that if it is consistent with your duty & feelings towards a poor miserable retch that you will grant her a pardon (if not already done) and forward the same to me at Morganton."

Stokes, however, took no action on a pardon for Frankie Silver and he was soon off to the Indian Territory in what would become Oklahoma. A note on the back of one of the petitions says, "Petition in favor of Frances Silver/Burke/Not acted on/see petitions to Gov. Swain."

David Lowry Swain is one of the more fascinating and mysterious figures in the Frankie Silver story. He is the one man who finally could have saved Frankie from the gallows. Why he chose not to do that is an enduring mystery.

He was born January 4, 1801, on a farm along Beaverdam Creek (about two miles upstream from where the author of this book was born on another farm beside the same creek) near Asheville. His father was a curious man, born in Massachussets and then a resident of frontier Georgia before settling in Buncombe County where he went from being a farmer to making hats and served as a justice of the peace, town comissioner and trustee of the local academy. His mother was Caroline Lane, daughter of a prominent eastern North Carolina family. The father instilled in the son a desire for education and a love of history for which all North Carolinians can now be thankful.

David L. Swain was admitted to the bar in 1823. In 1826, he married Eleanor White, whose father, William White, had been secretary of state, and whose mother, Anna Caswell, was the daughter of North Carolina's Revolutionary War governor, Richard Caswell. It was an important political connection to the eastern part of the state in those days when East and West were often bitterly divided.

At 21, Swain went off to the University of North Carolina and was accepted as a junior. However, he left after only one week and studied law under Chief Justice John Louis Taylor in Raleigh. He returned to Asheville in 1823 and the voters in Buncombe County sent him to the House of Commons for the next four years. In 1827, the General Assembly named him solicitor for the northeastern circuit; however, he resigned before the year was out and returned home to Asheville to be with his ailing father. He was elected to the House of Commons in 1828 and 1829. In 1830, he was named a judge of the superior court and was serving in that position in December 1832 when the General Assembly elected him to serve a one-year term as governor.

Historian Carolyn Wallace, longtime director of the Southern Historical Collection, studied Swain's life and work for many years. She even managed to decipher his all but impossible handwriting. Although she never published a full biography of Swain, she did write one of the longest entries in William Powell's Dictionary of North Carolina Biography on Swain. He had been a surprise choice for governor, a compromise by the warring factions against the leading Democratic candidate.

Wallace writes: "Swain thus had no hope of effective party support during his term. The governor's powers and duties were slight, and he was expected to be largely a social figurehead. Even for that limited position, Swain seemed poorly endowed, for his face was long and homely, his slender figure ill-shaped and ungainly, and his movements awkward. His advantages were an imposing height of six feet two inches, a kindly and intelligent face, and a courteous, genial, and witty personality that made him a welcome companion. In addition, he was considered a well-prepared, persuasive debater and public speaker."

In spite of the limitations of the job, Swain managed to set the ball in motion for state aid to build the first railroads and he was a major force for constitutional reform, serving as a delegate to the convention of 1835 which re-wrote the state's constitution and, among other reforms, removed the disqualification of Roman Catholics from holding state office.

In a written address sent to the House of commons on November 19, 1833, Swain cited the crying need for legal reform in North Carolina. "Among the various subjects which will come before you, the revision of the whole body of our public statute laws may be mentioned as deeply entertaining to the community. The earliest statute in force in this State was enacted in the year 1235, in the reign of Henry the Third. Our revered Code as it is termed, commences with the provincial laws passed by the General Assembly which sat at Little River in 1715, omitting the entire legislation of the mother country with regard to the State, during a period of four hundred and ninety years, and embracing more than a hundred entire statutes or parts of statutes. Of these many relate to the criminal law of the country, several create capital felonies or punish capitally, offences that were previously subject to a milder penalty.... The truth is, that not only the source but the very existence of our Statute law, is, as remarked by an elegant writer, with regard to the common law, 'as undiscoverable as the sources of the Nile.' In such a state of things, the expounder of the Law alone is safe.... Competent judges entertain the opinion that the bulk of our statute books might be lessened at least one third, by a repeal of statutes which are in effect obsolete....

"Is it not strange, that our Revisal should exhibit to the citizen, various enactments to punish offences which cannot be committed, and conceal from his view innumerable penalties attached to actions, which he does not know to be wrong? It is submitted to your wisdom to determine whether a legal system so perplexed, intricate and uncertain, is suited to the genius of our institutions, and the character of our citizens."

As high sounding as all this seems, there was no real reform in the criminal code as the result of Swain's actions or of the Constitutional Convention of 1835. In fact, the vast number of crimes punishable by death was actually increased in the revised code of 1837. Most of these were aimed at "corruption" among slaves, no doubt a reaction to the Nat Turner Rebellion in Virginia in 1831. It was not until the Revised Code of 1855 that real reform would come to the criminal code in North Carolina. Among other changes, it would have allowed Frankie Silver to take the stand in her own defense. She had been dead for 22 years at that point, and it's doubtful her lawyer would have put her on the stand anyhow.

Swain faced a hostile legislature his last year as governor and the General Assembly elected the Democrat he'd defeated in 1832 to replace him. Swain did not want to go back to the practice of law and actively sought the position of president of the university. From January 1836 until his death on August 29, 1868, Swain lived in Chapel Hill and served as president.

Surely the most enduring legacy of Swain's tenure was the founding of the North Carolina Historical Society. He set about collecting all printed and handwritten materials that related to the history of our state. He was the sort of man who saved every laundry ticket. During the brief time Swain was studying at Chapel Hill and in Raleigh when he was 21, his father wrote to him by every stage that left Asheville, three times a week. Every letter was carefully saved. Even later, Swain saved letters from friends and relatives which documented his father's mental decline into insanity.

However, you will not find a single mention of the Frankie Silver case — not one scrap in all the thousands and thousands of pages of handwritten and typed documents which formed the nucleus of the current North Carolina Collection and the Southern Historical Collection at UNC Chapel Hill. I have spent hours and hours going through Swain's papers in a vain attempt to find some explanation as to why he refused to pardon Frankie Silver. Dr. Carolyn Wallace has assured me that she never once encountered Frankie Silver's name in her own more thorough studies of the Swain papers and she made no mention of the case in her own biography of Swain in the *North Carolina Dictionary of Biography*.

At the spring term of Burke County Superior Court in March of 1833, Frankie Silver was again sentenced to be hanged, this time on June 28, 1833. However, on May 18, she cut her hair short, dressed as a man and made a desperate attempt to escape her fate.

The Escape

As fanciful as it seems, the details handed down about Frankie's escape from the Burke County jail would appear to be based on fact.

In a letter to Gov. David L. Swain, her lawyer, Thomas Wilson, wrote that she had escaped on a Monday night and was recaptured and returned to jail eight days later.

In an earlier letter, Wilson had explained that Frankie had lost all hope after the Supreme Court denied her appeal and her execution was scheduled a second time. "Escape was then her only hope — That she effected by whatever means she will never disclose — She was retaken and again incarcerated."

From the newspaper accounts, Frankie made her escape on the night of May 18. It was boldly suggested that she had to have inside help because none of the locks had been tampered with and nothing was disturbed inside the jail. It is a fact that Frankie's jailer, or "gaoler" as he signed himself, John Maguire, signed not one but two of the petitions to get her pardoned. It is also a fact reported at the time that Frankie cut her hair short and dressed as a boy to make her escape.

Alfred Silver was certainly no witness to Frankie's escape, but he can be relied on to give the family's version of what was talked about at the time, and it is similar to the legend cited in Part I of this book. He said she got out of jail dressed as a man and was following her uncle's wagon on foot when the sheriff came upon the family group. The sheriff rode up to her and said "Frankie?" But she answered: "I thank you, sir, my name is Tommy." "Yes," her uncle put in, "Her name is Tommy." The sheriff arrested her and she was returned to jail. Except for the dialogue, Alfred's version of the story is borne out by contemporary newspaper accounts.

The *Carolina Watchman* reported on May 25, 1833: "Mrs. Sylvers, who was confined to the Burke jail for the murder of her husband some ten or twelve months since, and sentenced to be executed on the 27th of next month, made her escape on Tuesday night last. No doubt she received assistance from some person without, as all the locks on the doors were opened by false keys, and not the smallest thing broke."

On June 1, 1833, the *Watchman* reprinted the following story from the *Rutherfordton Spectator and Western Advertiser*: "Felon Apprehended. We learn that Mrs. Frances Silvers, whom we advertised last week as having escaped from Burke jail, a few days ago, was apprehended on Wednesday last, on Sandy run, in the Southeastern part of this county (Rutherford), and was taken back to jail. She was accompanying her uncle, a resident in Anson county, who had been for a short time engaged in peddling wares in Burke. She was dressed in a man's apparel and had cut her hair short. We learn that her father and uncle have both been committed to jail as accessories to her escape."

The *Star* newspaper in Raleigh reported even more details: "Frances Silvers, who was convicted of murdering and burning her husband, and sentenced to be executed on the 28th of this month, made her escape from the jail at Morganton, Burke County, on the night of the 18th ultimo, by the assistance of some person or persons; who entered the Jail by one of the basement story windows, and opened the doors leading to the prisoner's apartment by the aid of false keys. She was apprehended, a few days later, in Rutherford county, and taken back to jail. When taken, she was dressed in male apparel, with her hair cut short. Her father and uncle have been committed to jail, as accessories to her escape."

In a letter dated June 12 to the governor, Lawyer Wilson says three persons were bound over for helping in her escape — her father, uncle and a third not identified. Wilson also says, "I do not believe they can be convicted without her testimony."

This may be the source of the legend that Frankie's father yelled at her as she stood waiting to be hanged: "Die with it in ye." Maybe he was referring not to her crime but to his and his brother's own in aiding her escape. Her lawyer said Frankie had told him who her confederates were and he felt justice would be better served by making examples of them instead of her. But, apparently, this was never done. No record has been found to indicate anybody was ever punished for helping in Frankie's escape.

The Confessions

Back in jail after her failed escape, Frankie became convinced that all hope was lost. By June of 1833, she had been in jail almost 18 months. Her lawyer wrote the governor that she had been chained to the floor of a dungeon during much of this time.

Frankie obviously felt from the beginning that she should say nothing and let the state try to prove she had killed her husband. She apparently didn't understand that there were different degrees of murder. She sent for some of her friends and made a full confession.

From all we know, Frankie could not read or write. Both of her parents signed all documents with an X and Frankie's child, Nancy, grew to maturity and died without ever learning to read and write.

However, it is also obvious that somebody did write down this confession and showed it to other people. In a petition dated June 3, 1833, her lawyer and Samuel Hillman said they read that confession and felt that "the statement might have received a colouring from the individual who wrote it and by possibility that words might have been put in her mouth calculated to elicit answers which she gave. For the purpose of satisfying ourselves we repaired to the jail, heard her statement in her own language, carried her through a cross-examination and the result was a conviction upon our minds that the statement made in the presence of William C. Bevins and Thos. Wilson DS [deputy sheriff] is substantially true."

Three petitions to the governor, all dated June 3, 1833, began by saying: "The Undersigned citizens of Burke, having seen the confession of Francis Silver...."

Unfortunately, no copy has yet been found of this confession. It is not among the many letters and documents relating to the case in the letter-books and official files of Governor Swain.

In a letter to the governor dated June 3, 1833, Thomas Wilson says that Frankie lost all hope after her recapture. "Under the impending responsi-bility of passing from time into eternity she made a free and full disclosure of all the facts and circumstances attending this unhappy occurrence."

One would think that Frankie's foiled escape would have confirmed her guilt and turned people against her; however, it seems to have had the opposite effect. Following her return to jail, a flurry of letters and petitions even more urgent than previous ones urged the governor to pardon her.

At least 50 people (including two of my own great, great uncles, John and Thomas Young) who had not signed earlier petitions now came for-ward. One of the most distinguished signers was a lawyer named Samuel Hillman, who had no doubt been a close acquaintance of Gov. Swain when he had served as a judge.

According to a biography published in a Morganton newspaper, Hill-man was born in Massachusetts. He first taught school in Granville Coun-ty, N.C., then studied law under Judge Henderson. He settled in Morgan-ton in 1818 "and was very successful and promising for some years after-ward." He was obviously highly regarded at the time of Thomas Wilson's petition because he is clearly used to bolster Wilson's case for Frankie.

Wilson wrote: "We went to the jail and I beg leave to remark that S. Hill-man was at the time perfectly taken & at himself from a rigid examination & cross examination. We were all of the opinion that it was clearly a case of manslaughter if not Justifiable Homicide."

Among the June 3 petitions is a personal letter to the governor with the same date from a man named William F. Thomas of Brindletown: "Sir: You have been petitioned for to pardon of Mrs. Sylvers who has been con-demned to death for the murder of her husband and is now living under your respite. I did not sign the petition for her pardon believing her unwor-thy of Executive Clemency and seeing the public would not be satisfied with her pardon. But now I will assure you that public opinion is entirely changed & I am under the impression that nine tenth of the inhabitants of Burke County would cheerfully sign a petition & would rejoice at her par-don.

"That public indignation which at one time was so strong appears to be satisfied & now the belief is prevalent that she killed him in a fracous, that part of her confession is not doubted though the manner in which she disposed of him is not fully believed."

Thomas says in his letter that he has talked with any number of prominent citizens, including former governor Hutchings G. Burton, and they all favored a pardon but felt it was too late, that there was not enough time to get a response from the governor.

In fact, the mail from Morganton to Salem to Raleigh took only three to four days, but it ran only once a week. In an emergency, of course, the governor could easily have hired an "express" rider to hand deliver an urgent message — if he had wanted to do that. The governor obviously did not wish to pardon Frankie Silver and explained his reasons why in a letter to her lawyer dated May 3, 1833. Unfortunately, there is no copy of this letter in the governor's papers or in his personal files at UNC.

It could be that Swain had held to Gov. Stokes ultimatum that he would need the signatures of all 12 jurors before he pardoned her, and only seven signed the petitions. Or, it could be that Swain was simply a "strict constructionist" who did not find there was any legal reason to pardon her. We will never know unless a copy of that letter someday turns up.

In response to the governor, Thomas Wilson wrote on June 12, 1833: "Dear Sir: Yours of the 3rd of May was rec'd on the 5th of this Instant by the Buncombe mail. It will be treat[ed] as Confidential & private. I have showed it to no one except the father of the unfortunate retch who was the subject of your letter & that in order to put him on his guard that he need not trust to much to other & he having too that he would inform her of her imminent Danger."

It must have been at this time that the young lawyer Nicholas Woodfin "rode through the mountains for weeks" getting signatures on petitions. Several of the copies would appear to be in his handwriting. Although Woodfin's own name does not appear on any of the petitions — unless it is one of several signatures that have become smudged and indecipherable over the years — but the name of his future wife does appear in one of the most remarkable pages in the governor's papers.

This is a petition to Gov. Swain from the ladies of Burke and Buncombe Counties. It is an extraordinary document not just because of its strong wording, but also because the ladies who signed it had no more legal rights than Frankie did. They could not serve on juries, vote or hold public office and it was highly unusual for women at that time to involve themselves in any sort of public cause. The governor had already granted a respite of two weeks — until July 12, 1833 — for Frankie to "prepare herself" for death.

The ladies' petition is dated June 29, 1833, the day after Frankie was originally scheduled to die. It is quoted here in full:

> To his Excellency David L. Swain
> Governor of the State of North Carolina
> Your petitioners are fully sensible of the Delicacy of present-
> ing to you this petition. Yet they justify themselves by claiming
> as a duty peculiar to the Life to be allways on the side of mercy
> toward their fellow beings and to the female more particularly.
> The subject of this petition is an unfortunate Creature of our
> sex, Mrs. Frances Silvers, who was sentenced by our court to be
> executed on the last Friday in June but by your goodness was
> respited until the second Friday in July. We do not expect to refer
> you to any information in this that you are not already familiar-
> ly acquainted with unless it be the treatment of the unfortunate
> Creature received during the life of husband.
> We do not refer you to this with a view of justification but
> merely to reiterate the various unfortunate events that have tak-
> en place in the world in consequence of ill grounded abuse
> indecorous and insupportable treatment in which the creature
> now before your Excellency for mercy has contrary to the Law
> of God & and (sic) the Country yet so consistent with our nature
> been her own avenger.
> The husband of the unfortunate creature now before you we
> are informed, Sir, was one of that cast of mankind who are whol-
> ly dissolute of any of the feeling that is necessary to make a good
> Husband or parent — the neighborhood people are convinced
> that his treatment to her was both unbecoming and cruel very
> often and at the time too when female Delicacy would most for-
> bid it. He treated her with personal violence. He was said by all
> the neighborhood to have been a man who never made use of
> any exertions to Support either his wife or child which termi-
> nated as is frequently the case that those dutys Nature ordered
> and intended the husband to perform were thrown to her. His
> own relatives admit of his having been a lazy trifling man. It is
> also admitted by them that she was an industrious woman. But
> for the want of Grace Religion and Refinement she has commit-
> ted an act that she herself would have given a world to have

been able to call back. We refer you to her child who is an infant and needs the protection of a mother. We hope that your Excellency will extend to the unfortunate female all the mercy you can Even to a pardon. & wipe from the character of the female in this community the Stigma of a woman being hung under the gallows.

June 29, 1833

(signed)

M. Walton, Morganton	*Mary G. Erwin M—*
M.M. Walton do [ditto)	*Eliza G. Burgner Mor—*
Goodwin Boushnell	*Ann McDowell B-County*
E.M. Bouchelle Morganton	*Rebecca M'entire B-County*
E.W. Bouchelle Morganton	*Peggy Carson do*
Catherine Wilson Morganton	*Catherine Carson do*
Eunice Wilson Morganton	*Elmira Carson do*
Jane L. Tate do	*Matilda Carson*
Catherine E. Bevins do	*Eliza G. McDowell do*
Evilina S. Hughes do	*Margaret S. Collett do*
Flora Bowman	*Mary Deal*
Ann M. McKesson	*Harriet Smith*
Delia H. Erwin Burke County	*Lydia Womack*
Cecelia M. Erwin Burke County	*Matilda Erwin Belvidere*
Adeline R. Davidson Buncombe	*Catherine R. Gaither*
Harriett M. Davidson Buncombe	*Mary E. Erwin*
Lydia C.H. Roan Morganton	

Along with the ladies' petition was a letter dated June 30, 1833 from W.C. Bevins which explained it: "Mr. Stuard the father of the prisoner was advised by Col. John Carson as being a means by which he might possibly obtain a pardon together with others of the village to get up a petition among the ladies. The prisoner however knows nothing of it but is preparing for Death to this proceeding however I have not advised either for or against. The minds of the People seem to be very much softened in her behalf since the determination on your Behalf with regard to a pardon. I am requested by Mr. Stuard to ask your excellency to add an addition to her respite. He thinks he will be able to add new light on the subject and the people think if there are any ground upon which to add to time it might possible aid in the cause of Justice and Humanity."

Governor Swain's response was dated July 9, 1833. "Dear Sir: I have received your letter without date but post marked on the 3rd inst. together with the accompanying petition of a number of the most respectable Ladies of your Vicinity in behalf of the unfortunate Mrs. Silvers, who before this communication can reach you, will in all human probability have passed the boundary which separates us alike from the reproaches of enemies and the sympathies of friends. All that is now in my power to do is to Unite in the anxious wish which doubtless pervades the whole community to which she belongs, that she may find that mercy in Heaven which seemed to be necessarily denied upon earth, a free pardon for all the offenses in her life.

"I beg you to assure the fair petitioners, with the most of whom I have the pleasure of an acquaintance that the benevolent motives which influenced their memorial in behalf of the unfortunate convict, are duly appreciated and that no one can participate more deeply than I do in their sympathy for her melancholy fate."

Since the women's petition was clearly dated June 29 and the accompanying letter was clearly dated June 30, the governor was apparently trying to make a case that it had reached him too late for him to do anything to save Frankie from the gallows.

The Hanging

A fairly recent looking notation on one of the original documents still on file in the Burke County Clerk of Court's office says that Frankie Silver was hanged from an oak tree in John Dickson's front yard and that Dickson's property lay on Valdese Avenue somewhere between White Street and Broadoak Hospital.

However, I have not been able to find any sort of eyewitness accounts of the hanging. I pored over thousands of pages of letters and other documents in Morganton and the state archives and the Southern Historical Collection, where no less than 20 Burke County families' papers from that time are on file. There was news of the horse races out at Charles McDowell's Quaker Meadows plantation and of the frenzied activity in the various gold mines that were then being worked in the area. But I could find only one mention of the hanging.

This was in the coded diary of a young school teacher named William Prestwood. The diary was in code because it largely records the many sexual conquests of the teacher. When I found a copy of the diary that had been translated from the code in the North Carolina Collection at UNC-Chapel Hill, I excitedly turned to the date of the hanging, July 12, 1833. This is what I found: "Woman hanged."

The truth is there may not have been more than a handful of witnesses to the hanging. There is a very strong tradition in Morganton that the sheriff had a board fence constructed around the execution area. In an article published in the February 13, 1968 *Morganton News-Herald*, Geneva Hiergesell writes that a Mrs. Henry Morrow swore that her father, Reuben O. Phillips, was among the throng of people who crowded into town to see the hanging only to confront the board fence. "And Mrs. Morrow remembers his telling it time after time, how he had to take a pocket knife and cut a hole in a plank to be able to see Frankie as she hung with her hair cut short like a man's."

Also, there is at least one other example in North Carolina where tradition says a person was hanged "from an old oak tree" and, in fact, he was hanged from the beams of a scaffold. The reason is fairly obvious. Unless it's a mighty sturdy tree, the limb will give with the weight of the condemned person and the rope won't break his neck as it's supposed to do. My own opinion is that with all the construction going on — a jail just finished, a courthouse under construction — there was plenty of lumber and a scaffolding was the proper way to do it. Moreover, they had plenty of time to build a scaffold during the two-week respite Gov. Swain had granted Frankie.

That said, it should be remembered that the last woman hanged in North Carolina, in 1896, merely stood upon a crate. Somebody knocked the crate out from under her and that still didn't kill her so a man in the audience stepped forward and pulled her legs until she was dead. Still another writer has suggested Frankie may have been hanged from a wagon or cart, the way they did in the wild wild West — or at least the movies about the West — with the vehicle pulled out from under at the moment of death. But that is yet more speculation too many years after the fact.

Did 10,000 people turn out to watch the hanging, as more recent accounts tell us? Who knows? With no eyewitness reports from that time (and that, in itself, is curious) there is honestly no way to know. I at first doubted that figure because it represented far more than the entire population of the county, which was much larger in land size at that time.

But, while working in the North Carolina Archives recently, I came across a genuine eyewitness account of a double hanging in Asheville just two years after Frankie Silver was hanged. Two men named James Sneed and James Henry had been convicted of horse stealing, doubtless the most common capital offense in those days when horses were so vital to one's life and livelihood. This account was written by Allen Turner Davidson, who was born on May 9, 1819, and died January 24, 1905, after a long and distinguished career as a lawyer in Asheville. His account of the hangings in 1835 gives us a fairly good idea of what might have taken place in Morganton in 1833.

Davidson was 16 at the time of the hangings. He had walked into

Asheville from his father's farm in Haywood County the day before and managed to get a space at the old Buck Hotel, sharing a pallet with another man in the hotel's attic. The morning of May 28, 1835, Davidson woke up before daylight.

"I wasted no time in making my simple toilet, but imediately struck out for the street. The whole front and public square were covered with people. It was only just about day light then. The people had not slept much the previous night. The excitment was intense. People must have been coming in all during the night.... It was impossible to get near the jail to see the prisoners because of the crowd and the guard.... The crowd was estimated by men of judgment at from 5,000 to 8,000. It must be remembered that there were few wheels in the country then, and most people came on foot or on horse back. Many came from long distances...."

Davidson wrote that the scaffold for the hanging had been built near where present day Merrimon Avenue intersects with Broadway and Lexington Avenue in Asheville. "There stood the gallows, grim and forbidding. The beam from which the ropes were to dangle was in place and the trapdoors were there too, and the steps leading to the platform. There was a double grave half finished on the hill near by.... At about two o'clock it started...here they came, thousands of eager and excited people, and the prisoners seated on their coffins in a wagon surrounded by the military. They drew up at the foot of the gallows, and several people mounted the scaffold with the prisoners. There were two long sermons.... There was praying and excitement of the most intense character.... The prisoners were then given an opportunity to make any remarks they desired to make."

The first to speak was James Sneed, a "clean shaven fine looking young man," who said "he had been a wild, wicked young man, and was an adventurer, making money by every turn and was not slow to use his profession in tricks at cards to procure money from the ignorant and unsuspecting but that he had done nothing to deserve death. He had never taken human life and had never taken any man's property by force." James Henry spoke next. Davidson described him as "a heavy headed, thick shouldered strong man. He impressed me by his general look and demeanor as a man capable of committing any crime."

Although Davidson did not hear the exchange himself, one of the militia guards up close to the scaffold, Pleas. Israel, later told him that Henry challenged his accuser to come forward and admit he had lied. However, the man "walked off sulkily without stating how it was."

Davidson concludes his account: "Then the end came. The black caps were drawn over the faces of the two men, the sheriff and his deputy bade the men good bye, and retired from the trap. The signal was given, and then happened a thing, just for an instant only, like a flash of light, that I have never forgotten. The trap, which consisted of two doors meeting in the middle and working from the sides on hinges, fell at first with a great crash as the trigger was knocked out. But they did not fall clear down, but only part of the way, so that it was possible for a very short space of time for the men to touch them with their shoes. This they did repeatedly, trying to regain a foothold, but the doors were soon entirely beyond their reach, and they were fairly suspended. But I can still hear those poor feet in their blind effort to cling yet a little longer to earth."

There is one other fascinating aspect to Davidson's account of the hanging that took place in Asheville that relates directly to the earlier hanging of Frankie Silver. Davidson wrote: "I remember distinctly to have seen the evening before in the parlor of the Buck hotel Gov. David L. Swain, who was then governor, and who had been pressed to respite the prisoners to look further into the justice of the execution or for a pardon outright, but the governor left in the stage before day that morning and was not present at the hanging. I heard of a petition being circulated by Mrs. Perkins, a sister of James W. Patton, for the pardon of the prisoners, and there was one expression in it which I have remembered ever since. It was to the effect that no son of a woman should suffer the death penalty for the foal of an ass. Gov. Swain was censured for leaving when he did by those who wanted a pardon or respite."

You have to ask yourself why no such eyewitness accounts were passed down about what would have been the much more sensational hanging of a woman. The most obvious explanation is that no eyewitness details were passed down because there were no eyewitnesses — or, at least, only a very small number; maybe only the sheriff and the executioner himself. We have only some vague details about the hanging contained in two very brief newspaper notices.

Unfortunately, the most detailed account was in the July 27, 1833, *Miners' and Farmers' Journal* of Charlotte, and several words are impossible to read. The words in brackets are my own educated guess as to what those words might have been. "Frances Silvers who was sentenced [to be] hung in Burke County for the murder [of her] husband, was executed on the 12th [ultimo or last]. She made a full confession before two [lawy]ers which she confirmed under the [gallows] before she was executed. The con[fession] has been published, from which we [learn] that at the time of the murder Silvers [was in] the act of loading his gun to shoot [his wife], whose life he had threatened."

On August 2, 1833, *The Star, And North Carolina Gazette* in Raleigh reported: "Frances Silvers was hung at Morganton, Burke County, on the 12th ultimo for the murder of her husband, Charles Silvers. Previous to her execution, she made a full confession of the crime for which she suffered."

The myth that Frankie Silver sang or read a ballad from the gallows is no doubt the result of the fact that she had made a confession not once but twice in her jail cell, and "confirmed" it from under the gallows just before she was hanged. The confusion was strengthened by the fact that — as Alfred Silver confirmed — the ballad or "Confession" (actually written by a school teacher named Thomas W. Scott) was printed on slips of paper and sold at the hanging. The story of the ballad Frankie never sang is explained in more detail in Part III of this book.

The Burial

As with nearly every other detail of the Frankie Silver case, there are dozens of conflicting stories about where and how she was buried. As with the hanging itself, there are no eyewitness accounts dating from that time.

According to one legend, Frankie's father was fearful that her body would be claimed by medical students. They normally got the cadavers of condemned men and would have a rare chance to study the body of a woman. But, since there was no medical school in the state at that time, this sounds very farfetched. This and other stories suggest that the father dug several false graves in order to keep the curious away from the real place where he buried his daughter.

For most of this century, the accepted story in Morganton and Burke County is the one recited in Part I: That Frankie's family took the body and were headed home to the Toe River on the old Yellow Mountain Road, the original trading path and road from Morganton across the mountains to the first settlements in Tennessee. It was mid-July, of course, and the body began to decompose fairly quickly in the heat. The Stewarts stopped at the old Buckhorn Tavern, about eight miles north of Morganton and stayed the night, with Frankie's casket resting in an old shed out front of the big two-story log house built by William Alexander around 1812.

The Alexander House or Buckhorn Tavern stood well into this century and was described in detail in a 1931 article in the *Morganton News-Herald* as the oldest wooden building in the county. The fireplaces were so big they could burn logs up to four feet long. Frank DeVault was the chief source of information for the article and said his mother had been born in the old house in 1825. His father was Jake DeVault from Fordtown, Tennessee, a stock driver who stopped at the tavern, fell in love with one of the Alexander daughters and married her on July 21, 1853. The Buckhorn Tavern stayed in business until 1881, and the DeVaults eventually inherited the property. It had once consisted of 1,400 acres, but in 1931, Rufus Carswell owned the house and 142 acres surrounding it.

This is how Geneva Hiergesell told another story about the burial in an article published in the January 21, 1968, *Asheville Citizen-Times*: "Early on a hot July morning in the year 1832 [sic], a little girl stopped her play to watch a wagon bearing a heavy load and guarded by strange and grim looking men on horse back lumbered up the Yellow Gap road in Burke County, coming from the Buckhorn Tavern toward the old Devault place.... As the little girl watched, the men stopped, conferred, and turned off the main road, driving and pushing and straining to get the wagon with its jostling oblong heavy load up the bank and into the secrecy of the woods.

"The little girl crept nearer, but the grim faced men and the lone woman paid her no attention. They were busy selecting a spot at the top of a knoll, digging a hole, tearing away bushes, measuring the box, digging again, all in voiceless silence.

"Then, the grave completed, the men lifted the box from the wagon, with much straining and the only sound which could be heard above the buzzing of the bees and the singing of the birds and the rustling of the leaves in the hot, summer air, was the sobbing of the lone woman.

"From her bonnet covered face there came sounds the like of which the little girl had never heard before. Then it was the woman spoke, begging that the box be opened for one last look. The younger men said no, there was not time, but the older man looked with kindness and compassion on the woman's face and took a crow bar and ripped the silence of the woods, as he tore the lid from the home made box.

"The little girl took one look, then she could see and smell no more. For she had fainted. Many a time has Frank Devault sat at the kitchen table in the home of the Rev. Rob Harris who lives near the grave of Frankie Silvers and told about the day his mother, when she was a little girl, saw the Stuart family bury the only woman ever hanged by her neck in Burke County."

Lush — if ungrammatical — as these details are, they are no more reliable than the last statement that Frankie was the only woman hanged in Burke.

Now, I was all ready to accept that story. I mean, who's to say the history we read in newspapers isn't true? But, then, I got a letter from Mrs. Charles Stanton Jr. of Asheville. She wrote: "My father was Ray DeVault. When I was a child, my parents would visit the uncles on the DeVault farm located along the Catawba River. I was told that Uncle Frank DeVault made the casket for Frankie Silver and understood she was buried on the edge of the farm. Of course, all of these people are dead now but I do remember the stories about her death. Other articles have been written about a little girl watching the burial. The little girl would have been Nan DeVault. She told me that was not true."

Like many other aspects of the Frankie Silver story, we cannot say for sure just where she was buried. In the absence of any factual documentation, it must remain a mystery. And maybe that's exactly how old Isaiah Stewart wanted it to be.

However true Frank DeVault's memory of his mother's little girl story, it was this memory that helped locate the grave site for the handsome marble tombstone that finally gives some sort of monument to Frankie Silver, complete with the usual misspellings and misstatements of facts: "FRANKIE SILVERS [sic] ONLY WOMAN EVER HANGED IN BURKE COUNTY HANGED AT MORGANTON JULY 12, 1833." The marker was placed at the site just off U.S. 126 about eight or nine miles north of Morganton in 1952 by Beatrice Cobb, owner and publisher of the *Morganton News-Herald* for many years.

I regret that Beatrice Cobb, whose newspaper did more than any other to get at the facts of the Frankie Silver case, did not live to see this book published and all the new information it contains. I would hope that the inscription will someday be re-carved to reflect Frankie's true place in history. Her story was dramatic enough without the "first" or "only" qualifiers so many storytellers seemed to think it needed to make it interesting.

Frankie's Child

Lost to nearly everybody except the women petitioners, of course, was the fact that this accused murderer was also a mother with a baby girl not yet old enough to walk. The late Larry Wood insisted there was a very strong tradition among the Stewarts in Macon County that Frankie's daughter was spirited over to them for safekeeping during and after the trial. However, there is no documentation for this.

Little Nancy's name first appears in the record in the minutes for the April 1836 Court of Common Pleas and Quarter Sessions of Burke County. Justices of the Peace James Avery, R.C. Pearson and John Collett ordered the following: "Ordered by the court that Nancy Silver, an orphan daughter of Francis Silver, deceased, being about five years old the 3rd day of November 1835, be bound unto Barbara Stuart until she is eighteen years of age; to receive at her freedom one cow and calf, two suits of clothes, one good bed and furniture and twelve months schooling."

Now, there is also a very strong tradition among the Silvers that Frankie's daughter was raised by them, but again, there is no documentation for this claim. In H.E.C. Bryant's interview of Alfred Silver published in 1903, he said that "Nancy, the daughter of Charles and Franky Silver, grew into womanhood and married David Parker, who died fighting for the Confederacy at the first battle of Manassas. The widow married again and is now said to be living in Madison County."

Nancy Silver was not listed in the household of Blackstone Stewart in the 1850 census, although her grandmother, Barbara Stewart was there. I looked in vain for her name in the various households of relatives but never did find her. By 1860, however, she was married and the mother of four children.

The 1860 census shows that David and Nancy Parker owned the farm nextdoor to Nancy's wealthiest Silver relation, Green or Greenberry Silver, who listed his personal and real property as valued at $10,000 each, a handsome sum at that time and place. The Parkers were not that well off, but with real property valued at $257 and personal property at $250 neither were they as poor as her parents had been.

They lived in the Ledger area of Yancey County. Their six children were: 1. Jacob William Parker, born September 7, 1852; 2. Charles Westley Parker, born September 13, 1854; 3. Rhinetter or Phinetter Elizabeth Parker,born April 27, 1857; 4. Margaret Alice Parker, born February 1, 1859; 5. Magdalina Mariah Parker, born March 1, 1861; and 6. Cansada or Kansas Parker, born July 29, 1865.

We find David Parker's war record in Volume XIII of *North Carolina Troops, 1861-1865*, published in 1993 by the N.C. Department of Archives and History. A native of McDowell County, he enlisted on March 21, 1862, and served in Company B, 54th Regiment. He was captured during a battle at Rappahannock Station, Virginnia, on November 7, 1863, and confined to prison at Point Lookout, Maryland, from November 11, 1863, until he was paroled on March 15, 1864, in an exchange of prisoners. He was wounded in the forearm at New Market, Virginia, on September 24, 1864. He was hospitalized but returned to duty. On March 28, 1865, he was wounded again, this time a gunshot wound in the right thigh — the place and date not specified — and hospitalized in Richmond. He became a prisoner again when the hospital was overrun by Union forces on April 3, 1865. David Parker died in the hospital on April 14, 1865, five days after General Robert E. Lee's surrender at Appomattox Court House.

Times were hard for everybody in the South during the Civil War and the years just following it. However, the people in the mountains were especially hard hit. Like the Parkers, most of them had owned no slaves and enjoyed no benefits from the politics of either side of the war. Raiders from the armies of both sides would sweep through and take whatever the poor people had. And, in between the official acts of plunder, roving bands of renegades would ride through and terrorize the people just for the hell of it.

"Hit don't matter who wins the war, we're gonna lose," said one old fellow in Yancey County. And Frankie's daughter lost all she had. With everything of value stolen by the raiders and with no husband to help with the farm, she soon lost the property and had to farm the children out to various ones who would give them bed and board in exchange for work on their farms.

I was never able to find Nancy in the 1870 census. Possibly because of her Stewart relations, the widow Parker moved to Macon County about that time and on January 10, 1872, she married William C. Robinson at Franklin. They would have one child, a son named Commodore Robinson. All of Nancy's children would stay and marry in Macon County, except for Margaret Alice Parker, who would marry John Henry McKamey ("Mack") Thomas and move back to the Toe River area where her grandmother Frankie had once lived. (Further details on the descendants of Frankie Silver are at the end of Part IV.) When Nancy Parker Robinson died on September 30, 1901, she was buried in the Mount Grove Cemetery in Macon County. For some reason, her tombstone was engraved with the name Nancy Parker instead of Robinson. Her children by Parker were all fiercely proud that their father had fought and died for the Confederacy.

According to her descendants, Alice Parker Thomas was estranged from her mother because she blamed her for losing the farm and not holding the family together in those terrible years following the war. One of her sisters and her half-brother visited her once, but her descendants think that other than that, there was no contact between her and her family in Macon County.

Her grandmother was involved in the most sensational crime of the 19th century in the Toe River Valley, and by some cruel turn of fate, Alice Thomas would become the victim of the most sensational crime in Mitchell County in this century.

Just after noon on September 26, 1923, Mrs. Thomas set out from her house to go see her husband who was working some distance away. She was about a half mile from home, near the house of Milissy (or Melvira, as the name appears in some accounts) Silver. Mrs. Thomas was coming down from the Silver's house when she met up with a black man later identified as John Goss. At first the man asked her for a glass of milk. Mrs. Thomas continued on down the hill, but the man waded through mud and got in front of her. He pulled out a large pocket knife, grabbed her and told her he would cut her throat if she said anything. Then he raped her and told her to wait there for a half hour while he made his escape.

Goss was an illiterate prisoner who had been transferred to the mountains from New Hanover County to work on road construction in Mitchell

County. He was part of a "trusty" program for well-behaved prisoners and had no previous marks against him. As soon as she felt safe to run, Mrs. Thomas found her son and he alerted the rest of the family.

All they knew was that a black man had raped a white woman, and panic quickly spread through the coves and valleys of the steep mountains. A white mob estimated at 200 rounded up all the blacks in the county, stopped a freight train and forced the blacks to get into two cars bound for Spartanburg, S.C.

The mayor of Spruce Pine sent a telegram to Gov. Cameron Morrison that blacks were being forcibly removed from the county. Morrison immediately sent the state adjutant general to Spruce Pine and issued a statement saying he would "afford the community ample protection, in order to safeguard the rights of all its citizens, both white and colored." He sent a telegram to the mayor saying: "Please call on local authorities to uphold the law and protect everybody in their rights including the colored people."

Meanwhile, a posse of 75 white men combed the mountains for the assailant they knew only as a "colored man." As soon as the adjutant general arrived in town, he ordered units of the National Guard into Spruce Pine and the town became an armed camp. Machine guns were mounted on the south side of the Toe River and trained on the main business district. Roughly 250 black citizens had been removed from their construction and mining jobs and their white bosses protested to the governor that these were good, law abiding citizens.

The white posse tracked Goss to a railroad overpass at Drexel in Burke County, where apparently he had hopped a freight train to Hickory. On September 29, 1923, the police chief in Hickory spotted a black man coming out of a house eating cheese and crackers. He promptly arrested him and determined his name was John Goss.

Since he was a prison escapee, Goss could be held without a warrant and he was promptly sent to the state prison in Raleigh. Mrs. Thomas and her husband went by train to Raleigh where she identified Goss as her assailant. Governor Morrison promptly ordered a special court in Mitchell to try Goss on October 22.

Meanwhile, the Tri-County Fair at Spruce Pine went ahead as scheduled on October 2, under a special ordinance prohibiting the possession of firearms in public "in view of the riotous conditions due to recent unlawful acts on the part of certain citizens of Mitchell County...." The troops still stationed in the town put on a show and won the hearts of the fairgoers with an equestrian demonstration that featured one man riding four horses.

The governor saw to it that a heavy military guard escorted the prisoner to Mitchell County for the trial. When local folks beheld the man who'd caused all the ruckus they were amazed. One said, "He was the least little man I have ever seen." Goss' prison record shows he stood only five feet four inches high and weighed 145 pounds. More than 600 people crowded the streets of the tiny county seat, Bakersville, to see the little man led to court, weighed down by chains from his neck to his ankles.

According to a detailed account of the crime and trial published in the *Mitchell County News-Journal* by the current District Attorney in the area, Tom Rusher, the testimony against John Goss lasted only 30 minutes. From the judge's notes, on file in the county courthouse, it would appear that the rape itself was described only as "the act." Mrs. Thomas said there was no way she could be mistaken about Goss. Her neighbor, Mrs. Silver, was asked if Goss was the man she had seen just before Mrs. Thomas was attacked. She replied: "That's the jock."

The entire trial was over within two hours. The jury took five minutes to declare Goss guilty. The judge sentenced that he "be put to death by electrocution."

After the trial, reporters talked with Goss, and he said he had made things right with God and did not want to appeal. Just one month later, on November 30, 1923, the warden at the state prison in Raleigh carried out the order that he "shall cause to pass through the body of John Goss (colored) a current of electricity of sufficient intensity to cause death, and the application of said current must be continued until the said John Goss (colored) is dead, dead, dead."

Meanwhile, 48 white men were arrested on charges of rioting. All pleaded guilty to two misdemeanor counts and were released on good behavior and payment of a $25 fine and court costs.

A grave injustice was done to the history of this incident and the law-abiding citizens of Mitchell County by Muriel Earley Sheppard in her account published in *Cabins in the Laurel*. "At least a hundred participants [sic] of the mob were tried for rioting, but were released with costs and small fines upon Chief Wright's petition for leniency. The mob had this in its favor. None of the Negroes had been killed, although they might easily have been wiped out. Through all the confusion of mob passion the people of Toe River had kept sight of their original purpose, to run the blacks out of the country. The state had carried its point and demonstrated that Negroes have a right in the mountains, but the hill people showed so unmistakably what their reception would be that since then the Negroes have not wanted to come up Toe River."

This is a bald faced misstatement of fact. Nearly all of those blacks who were forcibly removed were escorted back into Mitchell County within three days. The African-American citizens of Toe River who bear my own surname never left the area. And, if you go to the cemetery of my ancestor, Strawbridge Young, on a bluff overlooking the Toe River at Newdale, you will find former slaves Peter and Caroline Young and dozens of their descendants buried right alongside the whites.

Alice Parker Thomas was a feisty little woman, I suspect a lot like her famous grandmother, Frankie Silver. Showing the best of mountain spirits, she was never ashamed about talking of this incident which, after all, had been no fault of her own. She lived on until 1957 and is vividly recalled by her descendants.

Several photographs show her to have been a sprightly woman with fierce dark eyes and long strawberry blonde hair. Larry Biddix of Asheville was 11 years old when she — his great grandmother — died. "I can remember well her spending time at our house on Altapass Road in Spruce Pine. One of my most vivid memories of her is her hair. When undone, it was long enough to reach the floor when she was standing. I don't remember any gray in her hair. There was some white, but for the most part, it was a beautiful light golden color. Margaret Alice was blind at this time but had only to hear one's voice to know who they were. She was a woman of fairly small size, but also one of a very impressive bearing. She was stern but also gentle and always gave me a very warm secure feeling when I was with her."

The "Curse" on the Stewarts

The terrible fate of Alice Parker Thomas alone is enough to make you believe in some kind of curse on Frankie Stewart Silver and her family. And this is yet another unfortunate myth that has grown up around Frankie's story.

As Alfred Silver told it: "The surviving members of the Stewart family met violent deaths in one form or another. The old man, Franky's father, lost his life while cutting a rail tree; a limb struck him on the head and crushed out his brains. The mother died from the effects of a snake bite and was in great agony the last hours of her life. Jack, one of the brothers, was killed during the Civil War. Joe met a sudden death but I have forgotten the details concerning it. Blackstone went to Kentucky, stole a horse and was hanged for it. All went. It looks like God made away with them on purpose. I believe that they all conspired to kill Charles. It was a horrible deed. He was a fine fellow. We all loved him."

After Alfred's account was published in 1903, other newspaper accounts elaborated on his notion that there was a curse on the Stewarts. Some said both her parents were dead soon after Frankie died, but her mother was still alive nearly 20 years later, at the time of the 1850 census. Blackstone disappears from North Carolina records between 1850 and 1860, and I could never find his name in the indexes to Kentucky censuses. We know that Frankie's father, Isaiah Stewart, died in early 1836 because his wife, Barbara, went into court in April of that year to get her widow's allotment from his estate. (These records, too, can be found in Part IV.)

As for Frankie's brother Jack, or Jackson Stewart, he became one of the legendary bravest sheriffs Yancey County ever had. There are dozens of stories about how he could singlehandedly overcome the baddest of the bad guys in those rough days. He was an avid Confederate supporter and was overly fond of confiscating property such as horses needed for the war effort. The story goes that he had taken two horses that belonged to the Gouge family and they came after him, shot him off his horse and left him to die in the road. Now, if it was a curse that caused Jackson Stewart to be killed during the Civil War, it was a curse he unfortunately shared with several hundred thousand others.

For balance, I urge the reader to go back to that list of children of the Rev. Jacob Silver, the brothers and sisters of the late Charles Silver. Of the 13, six met with untimely deaths. Charles, as we know, was murdered by his wife. John and Marvel died of unspecified fevers. Milton died of typhoid fever. Reuben was killed by lightning. Edmund Drury Silver died from injuries he got from being thrown from a mule. If God had it in for the Stewarts, as Alfred claimed, He doesn't seem to have been too sparing of the Silvers, either.

I was curious about how it would be to grow up with an ancestor as notorious as Frankie Silver. So I wrote to several of her descendants and asked them about it. It is important to note that all of these were descendants of Frankie's granddaughter, Margaret Alice Parker Thomas, who was much closer to her husband's family and the Silvers than she was to her own mother and brothers and sisters.

Larry Biddix responded: "I did not learn of the Frankie Silver hanging until I was about thirteen or fourteen. As far as I can recall up to that point, the matter was never talked about. I was reading Sheppard's book, *Cabins in the Laurel*, and came across the story in that manner. It was then that I started to ask questions. Though I had never been told about the matter before, I was at that time informed of the whole story as my family knew it.

"My family maintained that Frankie killed Charlie out of spite. I do not share that opinion myself after other things that I later learned.... I knew early on that there was little truth as to the stories about the Stewart family members. Some of them ended in tragic ends but nothing uncommon for that time and way of life."

Peggy Thomas Young of Johnson City, Tennessee, said she first heard the Frankie Silver story when she was about 10 or 12. "I was told that he came home drinking from a long trip of hunting and woman chasing. He was known to be a ladies man. Like a drinking man, he was in an argumentative mood. He reached for his gun and she in return picked up the ax and hit him. My Dad used to tell me that they tracked her from the river edge back to the house. That she had walked backwards in her forward foot steps in the snow.

"I was led to believe that she was an abused wife, which was exceptional at that time. It was very hard on a young girl with a child to cope mentally in the woods by herself in the dead of winter. I heard that the Stewart Family met with accidental deaths. The Thomas family believed that they knew something and would not let her talk at her hanging."

Robert Buchanan of Asheville told me, "I have heard of the Frankie Silver case all my life. However, my great grandmother, Alice Parker Thomas, was more apt to speak of her father and his service in the Confederate Army than any other aspect of her childhood. When she did talk about the case, she espoused the innocence of Charles and the fiecely jealous Frankie.

"I was aware at an early age that Frankie Silver was my ancestor and how I was related to her. The Frankie Silver case was often talked about in school especially during classes which related to local history. Many of the teachers had Thomas Family connections and I'm sure they were aware of the relationship.

"I had never heard that there were those who felt there was a curse on the family. Only in recent years have I heard any mention of the self-defense theory. I only found out recently that petitions were signed asking for a pardon.

"Alice Parker Thomas expressed her feelings about her mother to my mother saying that the estrangement was due to the breakup of the family and the loss of the family property following the Civil War. My mother says that she knows of only two occasions when her grandmother had any contact with her family and that was a visit from Mariah Parker and a visit from Commodore Robinson during the 1940s. I never knew of any animosity between the Silvers and Nancy or her children. I do know that Alice Parker Thomas had a very strong relationship with the extended Thomas family, including those who had married into the Silver family."

In my letter to Spruce Pine attorney Lloyd Hise, Jr., I had asked if he was aware of the petitions trying to get a pardon for Frankie, or if he knew of people like me and the late Sen. Sam Ervin who strongly believed that Frankie would never have been hanged if all the evidence could have been presented to the jury. I had not taken into account the historic Republican politics of Mitchell County.

Hise wrote me that the story he'd always heard was the conventional one told by the Silver family.

"I never recall Margaret Alice or my grandfather ever saying anything complimentary about Frankie Silver or anything bad about Charlie Silver.

"I never heard of self defense or any motive favorable to Frankie. Charlie was always a fine, hardworking family man not deserving of such brutality. Charlie was always the victim. I first heard these stories as a young child, generally before bedtime at grandfather's or great grandma Alice's, but I never recall being told that Frankie was her grandmother. At some point, I figured that out on my own. Frankie was not an ancestor anyone told children about."

Hise wrote that as a child he'd been told the story of his grandmother's rape and the execution of John Goss. "As a boy I never doubted justice was done, although I cannot now see how he possibly got a fair trial.

"I look forward to your completed publication and your conclusions about Frankie's guilt or innocence. Unfortunately, most of Frankie's descendants who were also my ancestors would have little sympathy for your work and they had little sympathy for her. They would have believed both you and Senator Ervin to be wrong. But then they seldom agreed with Sam Ervin. He was a Democrat."

Morganton Now

If she is not quite a local version of Betsy Ross, Frankie Silver has all the same become a celebrated figure in the history of Morganton and Burke County. No longer is she the despised villain who chopped up her husband in a jealous rage. She has at long last become the subject of serious historical inquiry and any number of people now believe it was not just her husband who did her wrong, but history as well.

As early as the 1920s, the *Morganton News-Herald* had published the official court records of the Frankie Silver case and the booklet has been reprinted in recent years. The original documents, by the way, are still on file in a vault in the new county courthouse.

The local renewal of interest in Frankie Silver began sometime in the early 1970s. In 1970, Maxine McCall published a booklet called *They Won't Hang a Woman*, which was a kind of fictional version of Frankie's story based on thr facts McCall knew at that time. It was printed by the Burke County Schools and prepared in conjunction with the Burke County Cultural Heritage Project.

A dramatic reading of McCall's story was presented in the courtroom of the old courthouse in July of 1977. Cheryl Oxford, then a student at Western Piedmont Community College, played the part of Frankie and told the standing room only audience: "What I done was wrong. I know that now. I just made it worse for myself when I tried to hide it.... None of my crying and pleading did no good. They'd done judged and sentenced me right there...."

The *Hickory Daily Record* ran the following headline over its story of the event: "They Hanged Frankie Silver Again."

On July 12, 1983, the town commemorated the 150th anniversary of Frankie's hanging with another reading of the play on the old courthouse square. The local news report of the event incorrectly described Frankie as "the only free white woman hanged in Burke Couny." By that time, the program had been videotaped and broadcast by the UNC Center for Public Television at Chapel Hill.

In October of 1985, more than 200 people showed up at what is believed to be Frankie' s grave near the site of the old Buckhorn Tavern. As reported in the *Morganton News-Herald*, "A unique chapter of Burke County history came alive in a special way for more than 200 local residents Sunday afternoon as they journeyed to the grave of Frankie Silver — the first white woman hanged in North Carolina." The purpose of the visit, according to Katie Snyder, president of the Burke County Historical Society, was "to help spark an interest in local history."

The main speech at this event was given by Morganton attorney Bob Byrd, for many years a student of the Frankie Silver case. At his law office, which is shared with Sam Ervin's grandson and namesake, Sam J. Ervin IV, Byrd maintains his own archives on the Frankie Silver case and happily shares the information he's collected. Byrd told the crowd, "We really believe that her remains are buried here. This is indeed an historic site where we are standing."

Another play called *The Legend of Frankie Silver* was written by Howard Williams and presented at the Brewton-Parker College in Mount Vernon, Georgia, in 1997. A ballet has also been written by composer Panaiotis and choreographer Kathy Sharpe and presented throughout Europe and the U.S.

With a Swiss documentary film crew, Sharpe and Panaiotis visited the site in downtown Morganton where Frankie was supposed to have been hanged — near the corner of White Street and Valdese Avenue. Their ballet, *The Ballad of Frankie Silver*, was presented in Athens, Ga., as part of the arts festival that went along with the Olympic celebrations in Atlanta. (If you search the name Frankie Silver on the internet, you will find an advertisement for a CD of Panaiotis' work along with the inaccurate historical note that Frankie was the only woman ever hanged in North Carolina.)

Another play — also called *The Ballad of Frankie Silver* — sympathetic to Frankie was presented at Mars Hill College in August of 1977. It was written by Susan Graham Erwin, the widow of the late U.S. Rep. Joseph W. Erwin, brother of Sen. Sam Ervin. The story in the *Asheville Citizen* for

August 2, 1977, began: "The legend of Frankie Silver, a fair-haired Morganton beauty who became the only woman ever hanged by the State of North Carolina on July 12, 1833, has produced many folk tales and songs. But now, 144 years later, the only drama based on the historical event will have its world premiere Thursday by the Southern Appalachian Repertory Theater on the campus of Mars Hill College."

Erwin said her brother-in-law, Sam Ervin, "helped her with the legal research." Ms. Erwin unwittingly repeated several historical errors about the case: "I tried very hard to stick to what I thought was the true account. The version that I used was the one given by her lawyer, Nicholas Woodfin, who said her hanging was really a miscarriage of justice." Like Sen. Ervin himself, she did not know that the actual attorney for Frankie Silver was Ervin's own collateral ancestor, Thomas W. Wilson.

The most bizarre event regarding Frankie Silver was staged by a self-proclaimed witch named Joann Denton in 1994. Denton had previously made a name for herself in Morganton by staging her own funeral, running for mayor and successfully suing the city for not allowing her to march as a witch in the annual Christmas parade. On Friday 13, 1990, Witch Denton held a seance at Frankie's grave. As the Sunday *News Herald* reported, "Silvers [sic], the first woman to be hanged in North Carolina, probably would have wished she could have hung around for what transpired above her earthly remains Friday night. But, then, maybe she did."

Some 75 people endured a pouring summer rain, complete with thunder and lightning, to witness the seance. Dressed in black "out of respect for the dead," the witch read from the First Book of Samuel, Chapter 28 in which Saul seeks the spirit of Samuel and the group sang "Amazing Grace." Then Denton intoned: "Come spirit, come! Come spirit, come! Come spirit, come!

"Speak to us Frankie. We're trying to find out whether you killed your husband. Did you actually kill your husband? Tell us, Frankie Silvers, speak to us. Spirit of Frankie Silvers, speak to us. Did you kill your husband? Yes or no."

At this point, one of Denton's young disciples went into a trance. She knelt beside a table. She stretched her hands across the table and they suddenly began twitching, then moving frantically about the table. Denton proclaimed: "She denies."

To me, the most interesting and important development regarding the Frankie Silver case is taking place in the public schools in Burke County.

For several years, a study of the case has been a regular part of the course work in Jo Ball's eighth grade class at the Heritage Middle School. Ball herself is a firm believer that Frankie should never have been hanged. "After extensive research and studying of the N.C. Archives," she said Frankie was a victim of spousal abuse who killed her husband in self defense.

The various classes that have studied the Frankie Silver case have actually gone to the scene of the crime and re-staged the trial with all of the evidence now coming out. They also decided that it was high time the governor of North Carolina granted a pardon to the late Frankie Silver.

The students' petition for a pardon was sent to Gov. James B. Hunt in 1994 and was signed by 190 eighth grade students at Heritage Middle School. What they asked for was not an outright pardon, but a "pardon of forgiveness." The students said: "We understand the pardon would not include that Frances Silver was innocent, but instead would be a declaration that she was forgiven for the crime. This request is based on evidence uncovered in case papers from the North Carolina State Archives that strongly suggest wife abuse resulting in an act of self-defense and numerous trial irregularities."

Although Ball and her students claimed to have read the records in the archives, their research was apparently not that complete in that they incorrectly identified Nicholas Woodfin as Frankie's lawyer and the archives records clearly show he was not. "References were made by Nicholas W. Woodfin, lawyer of Frances Silver, stating 'the law at that time (1833) did not allow her (Frankie) to testify in court and she was convicted. If she could have told her story to the jury, the results would be different." It is yet another example of how a historical error once in print — in this case, in Kemp Battle's *Memories of an Old Time Tar Heel* — gets re-circulated time and time again.

At the end of their petition to Governor Hunt, Jo Ball's eighth grade class had said: "Please contact Mrs. Jo Ball, Language Arts Teacher, if any information is needed. Would you please contact us with regards to a hearing date with the Parole Commission."

But Jo Ball and her students never heard from the governor. For some reason, their petition got directed to a young assistant attorney general named Jeffrey Gray. Gray had unilaterally decided not to recommend that the governor issue a pardon of forgiveness as the students had requested.

But the first Jo Ball heard of this was in a videotape called *The Ballad of Frankie Silver*, which features folk singer Bobby McMillon. The film was produced and distributed by Tom Davenport of Delaplane, Virginia, but in association with Dr. Dan Patterson and the UNC Folklife Department. A respected professor of English at the University for many years, Patterson is credited with turning the UNC Folklife Collection into one of the best folklore collections in America.

However, my esteemed former professor of English had also unwittingly made some serious historical errors in the film which I pointed out to him. (To his credit, Patterson re-wrote the booklet that accompanied the film to point out these mistakes.) In particular, the young assistant attorney general is presented as the final word on the historical truth and is actually shown in the research room at the North Carolina Archives with his hands on the original documents relating to the Frankie Silver case. In a dozen different places in those documents, Thomas W. Wilson is clearly identfied as Frankie's lawyer, yet Jeffrey Gray speaks of Frankie's lawyer as Nicholas Woodfin. In very unlawyerlike fashion, Gray goes on to repeat all kinds of rumor and gossip handed down about the crime as if it were factual. He says that Charlie was a handsome man with a lot of women friends and Frankie was jealous. Even Charles Silver's own brother, Alfred, denied that.

I spoke by telephone with Jo Ball not long after she had received a complimentary copy of the videotape from Dr. Dan Patterson. She was furious. This was the first she had heard that the students' petition for a pardon of forgiveness had been denied not by the governor but by a young assistant attorney general. Her students were learning not only the hard realities of the Frankie Silver case, but also that the government still often turns a deaf ear to the petitions of its citizens. While learning how to use the system, they learned that the system sometimes doesn't work at all. Mrs. Ball vowed to renew the petition drive, this time involving adults in Burke County; maybe then the governor won't be able to ignore it.

Meanwhile, the students re-staged the trial of North Carolina v. Frances Stuart Silver. A jury was chosen from the audience of students and parents. And various students involved in the research project took the roles of Frankie, her lawyer, the prosecutor and the judge. This time, the young girl who played Frankie was allowed to take the stand in her own defense. She explained the tortures she'd endured as Frankie's wife and told how she had picked up the axe only after he tried to kill her.

The news report of the mock trial bore this headline in the April 30, 1994, *Morganton News-Herald*: "Frankie Silver found not guilty."

Of course, it was a little late to do the woman in question any good, but it was a refreshing turn in the long history of the Frankie Silver case. If eighth graders are taking an interest in history and trying to get beyond the colorful stories to the facts, we can believe the long cycles of misinformation may one day come to an end. I sure hope so.

Part III

Frankie's Song

The Ballad Frankie Never Sang from the Gallows

Unfortunately, the feminine nickname "Frankie" is so much a part of American folklore, we cannot hear it without immediately thinking of the song "Frankie and Johnny."

It is one of the most popular American folk ballads. There is scarcely an American alive who cannot recite at least a few lines about how Frankie shot her man "'cause he done her wrong."

This has caused no end of confusion regarding the Frankie Silver case, which is frequently claimed to be the source of the song. You need only listen carefully to the melody and the words to "Frankie and Johnny," however, to realize that it came out of a Mississippi delta black blues tradition.

Most folklorists agree that we will never know for sure the specific origins of the song. Many say that it was originally about "Frankie and Albert;" still others think it was based on a real murder in St. Louis, Missouri, when a woman named Frankie Baker did, in fact, kill her man, Allen, because he was fooling around. In a book called, *Native American Balladry*, published in 1964 by the American Folklore Society, G. Malcolm Laws Jr., gives the following background for the song:

"John Huston, author of the play, 'Frankie and Johnny' (New York, 1930) thinks that the song refers to the killing of Allen Britt by Frankie Baker which occurred in St. Louis in 1899. Al Britt was an 18-year-old black boy who lived with mulatto Frankie...George Milburn said in a letter to Vance Randolph, '...The Frankie song may have been applied to Frankie Baker's case, but there is ample evidence that the ballad was being sung in widely separated sections of the country long before 1899....' (Notes from Randolph II, 126). The ballad is sometimes known to folk singers as 'Frankie

Baker.' Many conflicting reports concerning the age and factual basis of this piece have been circulated but so far research has failed to settle its origin."

Among the papers of Morganton attorney Robert Byrd, who has long been an authority on the Frankie Silver case, is an old copy of the ballad written down by an Effie Allman of Route 5, Box 89, Morganton. Although Byrd knew nothing of the copy's history, it would appear to be at least 50-75 years old. It is reproduced here in full:

Frankey

1. *Frankey was a good girl as ever body knew.*
   She paid a hundred dollar bill for a suit of Albert's clothes.
   Because she loved him so; because she loved him so.

2. *Frankey went down to the bar room*
   she called for a glass of beer
   calling out to the bar room tender have you seen Albert here
   oh he's my man don't treat me right

3. *Bartner [sic] says to Frankey little girl*
   I can not lie Albert left here a moment ago
   with a girl named Alice Frie
   if he's your man don't treat you right

4. *Frankey went down to the pool room*
   She started in at the door
   there she saw her gambling man
   standing in the middle of the floor
   oh there's my man don't treat me right

5. *Frankey says to Albert I am not calling in fun*
   if you don't come to the one you love
   I will shoot you with your own gun
   for you're my man don't treat me right.

6. *Albert come around the table*
   he got down on his knees
   calling out to his loving wife don't shoot me Frankey please
   for I am your man don't treat you right

7. *On last thursday morning at half past nine o'clock*
    Frankey grabbed the forty four gun
    she fired the fatil [sic] shot
    she killed her man dident treat her right

8. *Turn me over Frankey turn me over slow*
    Pray don't tuch [sic] my wounded
    side for the bullet's a hurting me so.
    For you have killed your man didn't treat you right.

9. *People says to Frankey,*
    Frankey why don't you run
    don't you see the police a coming
    with a Forty Four smokeles [sic] gun.
    you have killed your man didn't treat you right.

10. *Frankey is in the court room*
    seated in a big arm chair
    there she is listening
    for the judge to say just give her ninety nine years
    for killing her man didn't treat her right.

11. *Judge addressed Jury Jury went away*
    Found her guilty in first degree
    for the murder of Albert Gray
    she killed her man didn't treat her right

12. *Frankey constained [sic] in Prison under a electric fan*
    she whispers low in her sisters ear
    Never love a gambling man
    what Ever you do want treat you right

13. *Frankey is dead and buried*
    She lies by Albert's side
    People erected a marble slab
    of these words at there [their] side
    he was a gambling man and she was his bride.

There was no connection whatsoever between the blues song about Frankie and Johnny and the more stylized Appalachian ballad about Frankie Silver's murder of her husband, Charles, which legend claims that she sang as her confession from the gallows. However, as recently as 1994, a local history was published which claimed that the song, "Frankie and Johnny" was derived from the story of Frankie and Charles Silver. In addition to the confusion of the two songs, I firmly believe that the more popular "Frankie and Johnny" has caused generations of ballad singers and storytellers to embellish the facts to make our Frankie's story fit the more sensational and traditional story of the jealous woman conniving to kill a two-timing, gallivanting husband.

There is no evidence whatsoever to support the claim that, like the other Frankie, Frankie Silver killed her man out of jealous revenge.

There is a ballad about Frankie Silver's murder, but unlike the more familiar "Frankie and Johnny" we know precisely how it came to be written. It is not an oral tradition like that of "Frankie and Johnny," but a very rare case of a written tradition in Appalachian folklore.

We know this because in early March of 1886, nearly 53 years after Frankie's hanging, the *Morganton Star* published the following article which was reprinted on March 24, 1886, in the *Lenoir Topic*.

"Francis [sic] Silvers' Confession

"We publish, by request, the following confession of Francis Silvers, who was hanged in this place on the 12th of July 1833, for the murder of her husband. Some of our readers will remember the facts of the case.

This dreadful, dark and dismal day
Has swept my glories all away,
My sun goes down, my days are past,
And I must leave this world at last.

Oh! Lord, what will become of me?
I am condemned you all now see,
To heaven or hell my soul must fly
All in a moment when I die.

Judge Daniel [sic] has my sentence pass'd.

Those prison walls I leave at last.
Nothing to cheer my drooping head
Until I'm numbered with the dead.

But oh! that Dreadful Judge I fear;
Shall I that awful sentence hear:
'Depart ye cursed down to hell
And forever there to dwell'?

I know that frightful ghosts I'll see
Gnawing their flesh in misery,
And then and there attended be
For murder in the first degree.

There shall I meet that mournful face
Whose blood I spilled upon this place:
With flaming eyes to me he'll say,
'Why did you take my life away?'

His feeble hands fell gently down.
His chattering tongue soon lost its sound,
To see his soul and body part
It strikes with terror to my heart.

I took his blooming days away,
Left him no time to God to pray,
And if his sins fall on his head
Must I not bear them in his stead?

The jealous thought that first gave strife
To make me take my husband's life,
For months and days I spent my time
Thinking how to commit this crime.

And on a dark and doleful night
I put his body out of sight,
With flames I tried him to consume,
But time would not admit it done.

You all see me and on me gaze.
Be careful how you spend your days,
And never commit this awful crime,
But try to serve your God in time.

My mind on solemn subjects roll;
My little child, God bless its soul!
All you that are of Adams race,
Let not my faults this child disgrace.

Farewell good people, you all now see
What my bad conduct's brought on me —
To die of shame and disgrace
Before this world of human race.

Somehow, a copy of this issue of the *Lenoir Topic* ended up in the hands of a man named Henry Spainhour, who was then living in the town of Lowell, Garrard County, Kentucky.

Spainhour wrote: "I take it upon myself to give you a piece of information that you may place in The Topic if you see proper, as I think it would be best to correct an error I see published in The Topic of the 24th March, last. It is the case of the confession of Frances Silvers. I was living in Morganton when she killed her husband and until she was hanged right in fair view of the place where I was at work. I had a chance to know all about the circumstance, and how this piece that is now published in The Topic was gotten up. Many years ago there was a man by the name of Beacham who killed another man by the name of Sharp, in Frankfort, this State [Kentucky]. He was condemned to be hanged. He composed a song that was called 'Beacham's Address.' There was a young man who came to Morganton from Lincoln County by the name of Wycough. He worked one year in the shop where I worked. He had learned the song that Beacham had composed and frequently sang it, so that I learned it but have forgotten part of it.... Thomas W. Scott, then living in Morganton, got of Wycough a copy of the forenamed Beacham's song, and from it composed the piece now in The Topic copied from the Morganton paper.... Now, after nearly 53 years, some person has gotten hold of Scott's piece, composed from Beacham's song, many verses and lines the very same as taken from

Beacham's, with others commingled and other additions, to make the thing look as dark as the ingenuity of man could devise, when there is not the slightest evidence that it was a premeditated murder, but a matter of an instant. If Scott is yet living he will certainly know that these statements are true, but I am persuaded that it could not have been him that had this put in the papers. Some person not acquainted with the facts must have done it. I consider it wrong to brand the dead with greater crimes than we believe they were guilty of. [Signed] Henry Spainhour."

All of the people mentioned in this letter can be verified independently. The index to the 1830 North Carolina census lists a Peter Spainhower in Burke County with quite a large family, of which Henry could have been a part.

Only two heads of household named Wycough are listed in the index to the 1830 census in North Carolina and both are indeed in Lincoln County. The surname does not appear in Burke until 1860 when a William Wycoff is listed along with his wife, Fanny, and seven children. This William Wycoff lists his age as 49 in 1860, which means he would have been only 12 or 13 at the time of Frankie Silver's hanging in Morganton.

Thomas W. Scott is listed as a schoolteacher, 34 years old, in the 1850 census. This means, he would have been 16 or 17 years old at the time of the trial. The 1850 census also lists his wife as Sarah, aged 28; and the following children: Jane, 11; Marshal, 9; James, 6; Lucius, 5; Corsinna, 4; and William, 1 month.

The Kentucky case Henry Spainhour refers to was one of the most famous American murder stories of the 19th century. It involved a woman named Ann Cook, a prominent former congressman and state senator named Col. Solomon P. Sharp, and a young lawyer named Jereboam Beauchamp, a name that was pronounced and often spelled, "Beacham."

In 1819, the Kentucky capital was scandalized by gossip of Sharp's affair with Miss Cook. She moved to her family's farm and lived in seclusion until she gave birth to Sharp's child The baby was stillborn. Ann Cook was furious when she heard that Col. Sharp was claiming that the baby was not his and that it was, in fact, a mulatto fathered by a black man.

Jereboam Beauchamp lived near the Cook family's farm and soon became involved with Ann, although she was 34 years old and he was only 18. She accepted his proposal of marriage, but only on condition that he avenge Col. Sharp's slander on her good name. They were married in 1824 and Beauchamp made several attempts to challenge the colonel to a duel, all of which Sharp managed to dodge. However, at 2 a.m. on November 6, 1825, Beauchamp went to Sharp's house and stabbed him to death.

It was the trial of the century in Kentucky. Detailed reports in the local newspapers were reprinted throughout America. Two men actually sat in court and made a daily transcript of every word spoken at the trial and this, too, was published. Beauchamp was convicted on May 19, 1826, and sentenced to be hanged.

The story became even more bizarre at this point. Beauchamp's wife was allowed to stay with him in his cell as he awaited execution. He wrote a poetic confession, describing his action not as a crime but an act of honor. Rather than a sinner bound for hell, he thought of himself as a noble man who would be rewarded in heaven for his good deeds. Mrs. Beauchamp was no literary slouch, either. She composed several poems and wrote voluminous letters to friends which, like his confession, were quickly rushed into print. After writing out a lengthy epitaph — which would be engraved on their tombstone — the two prepared to kill themselves with laudanum, a derivative of opium widely used in those days. When that did not work, they tried to stab themselves to death. Ann Cook Beauchamp did die as a result of the stabbing, but Jereboam lived on to meet his death by hanging. As requested, they were buried in each others' arms in a single casket.

The nation was caught up in the melodramatic details of this case. Edgar Allan Poe wrote a play about it called *Politan*. William Gilmore Simms wrote two novels about the case. One historian makes a convincing case that Herman Melville's novel *Pierre* was based on the Beauchamp-Sharp case. In 1950, Robert Penn Warren's fictional adapatation, *World Enough and Time*, was published. Warren said another author had given him a copy of *The Confessions of Jereboam Beauchamp*. Originally published just after the trial, this book of Beauchamp's poems and lengthy confession was republished by the University of Pennsylvania Press in 1966.

One ballad based on this case has been published in *The Beauchamp Tragedy*, a course book edited by Jules Zanger of Southern Illinois University and published by J.B. Lippincott Company. Here are the first lines:

Gentlemen and Ladies, I pray you lend an ear;
A very sad story you now shall quickly hear;
It was of a bold young lawyer lived in Kentucky state
Who on his own true lover with patience he did wait.

She told him she would marry him if he would avenge her heart
Of injury had been done her by one said Colonel Sharpe,
She said he had seduced her and brought her spirits low
'And without some satisfaction no pleasures can I know.'

There are 12 more verses to this ballad, but it seems clear that they have no relationship to the later ballad of Frankie Silver. Dr. Dan Patterson of the UNC Folklife Collection has spent a great deal of time trying to track down a copy of the original words to "Beacham's Address."

It is listed in A Syllabus of Kentucky Folk-Songs by Hubert G. Shearin and Josiah H. Combs, published by Transylvania Printing Company, Lexington, Ky., 1911. It is described as having a rhyme scheme of a-a-b-b — which means that each verse has four lines and that the first two and last two lines rhyme. Shearin and Combs describe the ballad in which "Beauchamp pictures the meeting of himself and the devil in hell." Unfortunately, the authors do not include the words to the ballad and Patterson has not been able to find a copy in any of the major American folklore collections. Historian Lloyd Bailey has pointed out that in all the poems known to have been written by Beauchamp himself, there is an a-b-a-b, or alternating rhyme scheme. He contends that what Wycough sang, and what the schoolteacher, Thomas Scott copied, was actually a ballad written by someone else about the Beauchamp case.

This was, of course, a classic use of folk ballads in our culture — to hold up the sinner as an example of what will happen if you do not follow the straight and narrow. In a booklet written to accompany a videotape of "The Ballad of Frankie Silver," which features folksinger Bobby McMillon, a native of the Kona area where the Silver murder took place, Patterson has written: "The significance of these details is not simply that they exonerate Frankie of the authorship of rather bad verse, but that both songs follow the venerable tradition of the 'criminal's farewell' or 'criminal's goodnight.' This kind of production began to appear in England during the sixteenth century, soon after publishers discovered the market for news stories printed on small single sheets of paper or broadsides ('song ballads,' traditional singers call such printed or manuscript song texts).... A high proportion of the British ballads surviving in the Appalachians in fact appeared in the seventeenth and eighteenth centuries on British broadsides."

We don't as yet have the words to this version of "Beacham's Address" and we do not have an original printed copy of the words transcribed by the school teacher in Morganton named Thomas W. Scott. Until and unless we find a copy of the Beacham ballad, we must accept on faith what Henry Spainhour said about Scott merely changing a word here and there and copying others verbatim from the original Kentucky song.

The earliest version that I have found is unfortunately only a fragment. It was among some old deeds owned by Mrs. Alma McCall Childers, who lives on property in North Cove, McDowell County, which her ancestor, Robert McCall, purchased in the early 1830s from the heirs of my ancestor, Thomas Young. Two verses of a ballad are scrawled on the back of a folded paper involving a land dispute which is dated June 10th, 1835. There is no date with the lines themselves. With no more than a fragment, it is impossible to tell if these lines are from the earlier Kentucky ballad or were those written by Thomas Scott in Morganton. However, there are significant differences in these words and those passed down as Frankie's ballad. The lines are here quoted in full:

1st O dredfull dark and fearefull Day —
How has my glory fled away
My sun goes down to rise no more
Who will my Dismal fate deplore

2d O lord what will bee com of mee
For Deth must sun [soon] my potion bee

Curiously, these poetic lines on the back of an old deed are followed by a list of names, the first of which is "Mr. Sam'l Tate — dead." Samuel Tate was foreman of the grand jury which indicted Frances Silver. Dan Patterson has pointed out that the above lines must not have been copied from a printed ballad because so many of the words are misspelled, spelled phonetically.

Other than this one fragment, there are some slight variations in the wording of the Frankie Silver ballad, even in the number of verses, but it is remarkable how — in a culture of oral traditions — this one has endured intact because it was written down from the beginning. Among the papers of attorney Bob Byrd, there is a Xerox copy of a very old handwritten version of the ballad. It is word for word exactly like the "confession" printed by the *Morganton Star* in 1886. It bears this inscription: "Written by a true friend, Katie Canipe."

Aside from the 1835 fragment, the earliest authenticated version we know about was found by Lawrence Wood in Macon County. It is in an old chap book, and bears this handwritten title page:

Written Feb. 15th 1865
Song Ballad for
Margaret A. Henry
Copied by James T. Henry

Here are the first two stanzas from this 1865 copy:

This dreadful dark and dismal day
Has swep my glories all away —
My sun goes down my days are past
And I must leave this world at last.

Oh, god what will become of me
I am condemed you all may see
To heaven or hell my soul must fly
All in one moment when I die

Among the same papers found by Wood, there was another copy of the ballad labeled: "Song Ballate." It is possible that this was copied in 1883 because that date appears on the front page of the chap book. Here are the first two verses from this copy:

This dreadful dark and dismal day
Has swep my glories all away.
The sun goes down my days are Past
And I must leave this world at last.

Oh god what will become of me?
I am condemed you all may see
To heaven or hell my soul must fly
All in one moment when I die.

Closer to the Silver home, a copy of the ballad was transcribed in 1946 by the local poet and historian, Monroe Thomas, for his uncle, Will Silver. Will Silver, who was born in 1876, was the son of David Ralph Silver, the younger brother of Charles Silver, who was born February 21, 1832, two months after Charles' death. The ancestral homeplace of the Silvers passed down from Jacob to David to Will Silver, who lived there until his death in 1961.

Born at Kona in 1903, Monroe Thomas was a remarkable man. Like Henry David Thoreau in Concord, Mass., Thomas had traveled widely in Kona. A graduate of the Yancey Collegiate Institute, he taught for five or six years in the one-room schoolhouses in Kona, Crabtree, Hawk and Altapass. By 1939, he was so severely afflicted with osteomylitis, he was forced to give up teaching and return to his parents' home at Kona, where he lived out his remaining 18 years. His body may have given out on him with this terrible disease, but Thomas' mind remained as sharp as ever. He read widely in history, psychology and the sciences. His most quoted poem was, incredibly, about "contentment." His bones and muscles had so deteriorated in his later years, Thomas could use only two fingers of one hand to write. It took him two hours to copy a single notebook page, and his amazingly neat precise handwriting is remarkably free of errors. Like some ancient scribe, he recorded all the old stories handed down in the area. He wrote detailed histories of the Silver, Thomas and Robinson families which have been carefully preserved by family members to this day. His brother, Walter, was Mitchell County schools superintendent for many years.

Wayne Silver, the current keeper of the vast Silver family museum and archives located in the two old church buildings at Kona, says it was Monroe Thomas who first put it in his head that there might be another side to the Frankie Silver story. It was only common sense, Silver told me, that there had to be a cause for a young woman to get so angry she would kill her husband. However, Thomas left no record of such an attitude. In a note attached to the copy he made for his Uncle Will Silver on October 18, 1946, Thomas said: "The above ballad was composed by Frances (Frankie) Silver while in jail and recited by her on the scaffold. She was hanged at Morganton, N.C., on the 12th day of July, 1833, for the murder of her husband Charles Silver. This copy made for W.C. Silver by Monroe Thomas from copy owned by Bryan Robinson of Bandana, N.C."

Bryan Robinson was the son of William A. Robinson and Emma Silver.

Emma Silver Robinson was the daughter of William Jacob Silver, younger half-brother of Charles Silver.

Except for two very minor changes, the copy by Monroe Thomas in 1946 is a verbatim copy of the ballad printed in the *Morganton Star* in 1886. However, it has two additional verses which were not published in the *Star*:

Awful, indeed, to think of death,
In perfect health to lose my breath.
Farewell, my friends, I bid you adieu
For vengeance on me must now pursue.

Great god! how shall I be forgiven!
Not fit for earth nor fit for heaven.
But little time to pray to God;
For now I try that awful road.

The ballad of Frankie Silver has a prominent place in the *Frank C. Brown Collection of North Carolina Folklore*, collected between 1912 and 1943 and published by the Duke University Press. Brown noted in his original papers that he got his copy of the ballad from a student named I.M. Pickens on September 22, 1922. Pickens said, "The following verses were handed down as having been delivered from the scaffold just before her execution." I quote only the first two stanzas:

This dreadful, dark and dismal day
Has swept all my glories away.
My sun goes down, my days are past,
And I must leave this world at last.

Oh, Lord, what will become of me?
I am condemned, you all now see.
To heaven or hell my soul must fly,
All in a moment when I die.

In her book, *American Murder Ballads and their Stories*, published by Oxford University Press in 1938, Olive Woolley Burt relies on the version of the ballad published by Muriel Early Sheppard in her book, *Cabins in the*

Laurel. Sheppard gives Frankie credit for "having some feeling, because in the last days of her imprisonment she contrived a long, gloomy poem which she recited from the scaffold before her execution." Since it derives more from an oral tradition, her lines are markedly different from others we have found. There is one similarity. Nearly all of them transposed the name of the judge from Donnell to Daniel. There seems to be an obvious explanation for this. Superior Court Judge John R. Donnell was not from the mountains. He lived in New Bern and his surname was not familiar in Western North Carolina. Daniel or Daniels was a more familiar name so later people hearing "Donnell" naturally assumed it was meant to be Daniel. Here are the first two verses of Sheppard's version of the Frankie Silver ballad:

> *On one dark and dreary night*
> *I put his body out of sight.*
> *To see his soul and body part*
> *It strikes with terror to my heart.*

> *I took his blooming days away,*
> *Left him no time to God to pray,*
> *And if sins fall on his head*
> *Must I not bear them in his stead?*

Muriel Early Sheppard also included a very long storytellers' rhyme about the Frankie Silver case. It is a kind of poor white version of black rap rhyming and I am frankly suspicious as to whether Sheppard ever heard such a thing. Both my parents were natives of Yancey County — my father was born there in 1889, my mother in 1910 — and I never once heard this kind of rhyming myself and never once heard my parents or any of their relatives or friends refer to any such thing. I asked Dr. Lloyd Bailey about the kind of rhyming Sheppard uses and he — a native and lifetime student of Yancey and Mitchell County history — says he never heard of such a tradition either.

Sheppard's version of the Frankie Silver case is told in a chapter called "Pole Cabins on the Toe" in *Cabins in the Laurel*. Sheppard explains, "In the mountains, nourished on the ballad tradition, verse, not prose, is the natural expression for a story, particularly a strongly rhymed, four-syllable measure. A practical joke, a wreck, a murder, anything that catches popular fancy and merits repitition, finds its way into verse." She describes Frankie's story as "an old story of jealousy and revenge, played out in a cabin in the Deyton Bend of Toe River, a story that keeps turning over and over and adding to itself like a snowball. There are half a dozen versions. Here is one recently told to an outsider, which will serve to introduce the story and show how a tale metamorphoses with oral repetition:

The Quiltin

Away up under a mountain top
Where the ravens wheel and the low clouds drop
Lived Charlie Silvers and Frankie, his wife,
A lonesome, hungry sort of life.
He was tall and broad shouldered and thin as a brier
But Frankie was small like tough hay wire.
He fished and hunted and cleared the field;
She sowed and hoed and saved the yield,
Picked berries and cooked and wove and spun
And mostly finished what he had begun.
The cabin was old and far too small,
Not much of a shelter from rain at all.
The corn field tilted against the sky,
The land was ragged and rough and dry,
Too far from town to sell the crop
Away up under the mountain top.
The woman hated the lonely place
And longed for the fields at the mountain's base.
From the high bare knolls she watched them lie
All neat and fertile under the sky.
And Frankie was jealous. She nagged and spied
While she thought Charlie courted; she worried and cried
When he slipped away, now two days, now four.
Each time he came back she hated him more.
One time he was gone almost a week
Somewhere yon side of Bandana Creek.
It was late and Frankie had gone to bed.
She heard his step and raised her head.

"Who is it?" she called. "I'm back!" said he,
"Back home again. Got a bite for me?"
She cooked what there was, side-meat and pone.
Not much in the cabin when she stayed alone.
He stretched out to warm by the fire on the floor
And dropped off to sleep. But Frankie before
She went back to bed sat thinking. She knew
He would always run off when he wanted to
And leave her alone. Well, she wouldn't stay.
She'd figure somehow to get away.
No one saw Charlie when he came.
If he disappeared, would she get the blame?
Close at hand the sharp axe stood.
She leaned above him. If she should —
The handle was heavy. The blade gleamed bright.
She brought it down with all her might.
Again! Again! She ran to the bed
And hid in the quilts till Charlie was dead.
So much was over and she had won,
But the horrible corpse — What must be done?
And gazing on him as he lay
She thought of a safe and awful way
To save herself and hide her crime,
To burn his body, a piece at a time.
And that she did, — all but his head;
She tied that up in a cloth instead.
It was too much Charlie to go in the grate.
You couldn't burn all of your lifelong mate.
But how to keep it? A ghastly sight.
She went outdoors. It was broad daylight
And the hollow stump of a sourwood tree
Yawned wide for Charlie hungrily.
She dopped him in. The deed was done
And where there were two there was only one.
One owned everything; one to spend,
One to sit worrying hours on end.
Day followed day — perhaps a week,
Then a boy came climbing the winding creek,

With word from Bertie McGuire, his mother,
If Frankie could get there some way or other,
She wished she'd come and help her quilt.
And Frankie was glad to go. The guilt
Of what she had done was mounting higher.
She'd eat cold food without a fire.
When she went out, all she could see
Was the hateful stump of the sourwood tree.
She went with the boy and forgot he was there,
Afraid on the mountain, she peered everywhere.
There were three of her friends at the quilting frame
In the midst of a ballad when Frankie came,
And Bertie said, "Come in and warm!"
With a friendly squeeze on her spindling arm.
The quilt on the poles was the Irish chain,
Of white and red liike a bright blood stain.
The women asked what she had to tell,
And she said, "Nothin'. I don't feel well."
And they all sympathized and 'lowed she looked bad
And reviewed all the sickness they had had.
She hardly spoke as the hours dragged through.
Just sat and sewed as she came to do.
As they rolled the poles for the last chain star,
The milch cow mooed at the cow pen bar.
Then Bertie got up and poked the fire,
And threw on pine so the blaze leaped higher,
And cut some bacon to fry out the fat
And put it to cook; got her man's old hat
And her working clothes to milk the cow
Out doors in the cold, and that was how
The bacon sizzled and frizzled and burned,
When it should have been watched and lifted and turned.
The guests quilted on till they smelled the smoke,
And commenced to sneeze and cough and choke.
A woman dropped her needle and ran
To snatch from the blaze the smoking pan.
They opened the door and fanned out the smell
As much as they could, and went out to tell

With laughter how they had talked so much
They forgot the bacon and fire and such,
But Frankie was silent and stayed behind
Distracted with something on her mind.
She sat on the hearth and held her head,
And thought of Charlie, burnt and dead,
And how his smoke had rolled and hung,
And curled and swirled and billowed and swung.
The same black smoke clouds in the air;
The same burnt smell was everywhere.
The hateful stench was making her sick.
She wanted to go and go right quick
And feared the smell would follow too;
She feared the woods that the trail wound through.
She dreaded the sight of the sourwood tree
Where Charlie's head waited gruesomely.
She feared the vengeance of the Lord
Might make her tell of her own accord.
If he cared enough to make her pay
He might have picked this special day
And caused Himself that burning smell,
To terrify, and make her tell.
The rest came back. She could not rise.
She did not dare to face their eyes.
Her wraps lay yonder on the bed,
But back at home was Charlie's head.
She could not stay. She dared not go.
She rocked, wild eyed, and cried, and so
At last she told how Charlie died,
And it came out, though no one spied
When piece by piece she fed the flame
With human flesh. The awful shame
Of Frankie's deed spread to every glen
Where stood the homes of mountain men.
Her friends forsook her. The Law stepped in
And Frankie hung for her heinous sin.
And they still tell when bacon's fried
Too long and scorched, how Charlie died.

To her credit, Sheppard included a footnote to the above that much of the rhymed stuff in her book was her own invention: "Because rhythm seems the natural form, I have put certain prose anecdotes into the strongly rhymed couplets of the countr...."

Although there is no factual evidence for Frankie's having acted because of jealousy, it is fascinating how this explanation took hold of the popular imagination and was passed down and repeated even among folksingers and storytellers like Bobby McMillon today.

Of course, Muriel Early Sheppard's main source of information was the Silver family and she never knew how loyal Frankie's own family was to her or that many of her close neighbors signed petitions trying to get her pardoned for her "heinous sin."

In 1953, Clifton K. Avery and the *Morganton News-Herald* included a copy of Frankie's ballad in a booklet entitled *Official Court Record of the Trial, Conviction and Execution of Francis Silvers, First Woman Hanged in North Carolina*. Their version follows verbatim the version published by the *Morganton Star* in 1886 It is preceded by these comments by Avery: "We are at a loss to know how Frankie behaved as she went to the scaffold, which was erected on a hill in what is now a beautiful residential section of the Town of Morganton. Nearly all of the stories handed down tell us that she repented and acknowledged her guilt. For many a decade there has periodically appeared in print a sad and doleful poem which she is reputed to have recited from the scaffold. It certainly shows a familiarity with the case and seems to have been written by some moderately literate person under a great mental or emotional strain."

It is an oversimplification to say that Frankie confessed her guilt before she was hanged. Once she explained to the sheriff and other witnesses that she had killed her husband because he was loading his gun to shoot her, the public sentiment turned in her favor and hundreds of people — including the clerk of court, her jailer, and seven of the 12 jurors — signed petitions asking for her to be pardoned. By then, of course, it was too late. Frankie might have been acquitted or convicted only of manslaughter if her lawyer had pleaded self defense.

Frankie obviously thought the only way to save herself was to say nothing, plead innocence. In the end, her own silence caused her to be hanged.

Illiterate, she could not write her own confession, so somebody else wrote it for her. And look what they've done to her song now.

Part IV

Documents

The News of the Day

There was no newspaper in Morganton or in Asheville at the time of Frankie Silver's trial; in fact, from all we know, there wasn't even a printing press in Morganton. There were only 21 newspapers in the whole state in 1830. In western North Carolina, the only towns that had newspapers were Salisbury and Rutherfordton. The *North Carolina Spectator & Western Advertiser* in Rutherfordton (published from 1830-1835) was the nearest to Morganton.

Stories about the trial were also published in the *Carolina Watchman* in Salisbury, which existed from 1832 to 1868, and from 1871 to 1898; in *The Miners' and Farmers' Journal*, which was published in Charlotte from September 27, 1830, until June 19, 1835; and in *The Star, And North Carolina Gazette*, which was published from November 3, 1808, until June 18, 1856, in Raleigh. *The Yadkin and Catawba Journal* was also published at Salisbury at the time of the trial, but no copies of the newspaper for the relevant dates are known to exist.

Very few copies of *The North Carolina Spectator & Western Advertiser* have survived. The North Carolina Collection at UNC-Chapel Hill has the most complete collection of original newspapers and microfilms of early newspapers in the state. The surviving issues of the *Spectator* for 1832 stop at February — which means that although there was an original account published in January about the crime, there is no way to tell if anything was printed about the trial itself. No copies exist for the year 1833, the year Frankie was hanged. The newspapers at that time all had exchanges with newspapers not just within the state but in the major cities of other states. They would often reprint articles out of other papers; in fact, that was their major source of news and information.

From *The North Carolina Spectator & Western Advertiser* of January 28, 1832 and *The Miners' and Farmers' Journal,* Charlotte, N.C., February 8, 1832:

HORRIBLE OUTRAGE
"_____ and bloody act is done;
The most arch deed of piteous massacre,
That ever yet this land was guilty of."

An occurence lately took place in Burke county, which has aroused the indignation of all classes of people — an occurrence which for terpitude can scarcely find an equal in the pages of fiction. The following particulars have been related to us by a gentleman who was lately near the place where the guilty and horrid deed was perpetrated. About 3 weeks since a Mr. ____ Silvers, who resided on Tow River, in Burke county, was missed, under the following circumstances. — -His wife went to the house of her husband, saying that he was not to be found at home, &c. She was told in reply, that he had been seen in the afternoon of the preceding day passing towards his own house, and had not been since seen by them. Hereupon, the family set off and tracked him (there being at that time a slight snow on the ground,) to home; but no track could be found to proceed from the house in any direction. The woods and river were searched by the neighbors, but without success. In the meantime the wife had packed up her effects and removed to the house of some neighbor. At length, some one in examining the fire-place, discovered human bones, nearly consumed, in the ashes! The search within and around the house was renewed. A portion of the body, partly consumed by fire, was found buried a short distance from the house — large puddles of blood were also discovered beneath the floor of the house, and in a bench was a deep gash made with an axe, together with blood, where to appearance, the head of the victim had been chopped off. It is said that the neighbors residing two or three miles distant, perceived a very strange and offensive odour in the air, at the time the body is supposed to have been burning. We understand the wife, together with another woman who is supposed to have been an accessory, were immediately secured and committed to jail, in Morganton, to await their trial at the next Superior Court. We do not learn that they have made any confession of guilt; but no doubt of the fact rests on the public mind. We are told that the wife had often declared to her husband and others that she would kill him. The deceased is represented to have been a man of rather vagrant and intemperate habits; and the wife as being the mother of one or two children. We forbear making further comments now.

The following two articles were copied from microfilm in the NCC Collection at UNC by Dan Olds of Spartanburg, S.C., in August of 1965:

From the *Carolina Watchman*, May 25, 1833:

Mrs. Sylvers, who was confined to Burke jail for the murder of her husband some ten or twelve months since, and sentenced to be executed on the 27th of next month, made her escape on Tuesday night last. No doubt she received assistance from some person without, as all the locks on the doors were opened by false keys, and not the smallest thing broke.

From the *Carolina Watchman*, Salisbury, N.C., as reprinted in *The North Carolina Spectator & Western Advertiser* June 1, 1833

Felon Apprehended. We learn that Mrs. Frances Silvers, whom we advertised last week as having escaped from Burke jail, a few days ago, was apprehended on Wednesday last, on Sandy Run, in the Southeastern part of this county, and was taken back to jail. She was accompanying her uncle, a resident in Anson county, who had been for a short time engaged in peddling wares in Burke. She was dressed in a man's apparel and had cut her hair short. We learn that her father and uncle have both been committed to jail as accessories to her escape.

From *The Star, And North Carolina Gazette*, Raleigh, N.C., June 7, 1833:

Frances Silvers, who was convicted of murdering and burning her husband, and sentenced to be executed on the 28th of this month, made her escape from the jail at Morganton, Burke county, on the night of the 18th ultimo, by the assistance of some person or persons; who entered the Jail by one of the basement story windows, and opened the doors leading to the prisoner's apartment by the aid of false keys. She was apprehended, a few days after, in Rutherford county, and taken back to jail. When taken, she was dressed in male apparel, with her hair cut short. Her father and uncle have been committed to jail, as accessories to her escape.

From *The Miners' and Farmers' Journal* for July 27, 1833:
(The first words on the left edge of the page are obscured in the microfilm print. I have inserted words in brackets which seem to fit.)

Frances Silvers who was sentenced [to be] hung in Burke County for the murder [of her] husband, was executed on the 12th [ultimo or last] She made a full confession before two [lawyers? The last letters are ...ers] which she confirmed under the [gallows?] before she was executed. The con[fession] has been published, from which we [learn] that at the time of the murder Silvers [was in] the act of loading his gun to shoot [his wife], whose life he had threatened.

From *The Star*, And North Carolina Gazette, Raleigh, N.C., August 2, 1833:

Frances Silvers was hung at Morganton, Burke county, on the 12th ultimo, for the murder of her husband, Charles Silvers. Previous to her execution, she made a full confession of the crime for which she suffered.

County Court Documents

The following transcriptions were made from copies of the original documents on file in the Burke County Clerk of Court's office in Morganton. Paper was a very expensive commodity in the days when these records were created, and the court officials wrote on every blank space, back and front, of every page. Two, three and often more documents were scrawled on the same pieces of paper.

Document #1
State of N Carolina
Burke County
     This day came Elighe green before me D D Baker an acting Justice of Sd county and made oath that in due form of Law that Franky Silver and Barbara Stuard [here the name "Joseph Stuard" has been crossed out] and Blackston Stuard is believed that they did murder Charles Silvers Contrary to law and against the dignty of the state sworn to and subscribed by me this 9 day of January 1832

             atest D D Baker JP   Elijah green

State of N Carolina
Burke County
     These are therefore to command some lawful officer to take the Bodies of the above named Franky Silvers, Barbary Stuard

[again, the name "Joseph Stuard" has been crossed out] and Blackston Stuard them Safely so that you have them befour me or some other Justis of Sd County to ansur the above charge and to be further delt with deanding [demanding] as the law directs given under my hand and seal this the 9 day of January 1832

D D Baker JP

[The following is written on what would have been the folded outside of the document.]

State
vs
Frances Silver
Recognizances

1/
The State
Vs
franky silver
Joseph Stuard [crossed out]
Blackston Stuard
Barbary Stuard
Executed Cost $1-20 Cts.
C Baker Const.
for the state 11 witnesses
for the Defendant 3
The cost of the warrant $1-20
for summons the witnes   3-00

———

$4-20

22nd Decr 1832
John Pagan [barely legible]

The Defendant Commited to Jael on the oath of Thomas Howel and William Hutchens Nancy Wilson Elender Silvers Margaret Silvers and Apon [upon] the word of the Jury given under my hand and seal this the 10 of January 1832

D D Baker JP

Document #2
The Indictment [Note: It is one sentence.]

State of North Carolina   Superior Court of Law
Burke County   Spring Term 1832

The jurors of the state upon their oath present that Frances Silver, Blackstone Stuart and Barbara Stuart all of said county, not having the fear of God before their eyes but being moved and seduced by the instigation of the devil on the twenty second day of December in the year of our Lord one thousand eight hundred and thirty one with force and arms in the county of Burke aforesaid in and upon one Charles Silver in the peace of God and of the State then and there being feloniously wilfully and with malice aforethought did make an assault; and that the said Frances Silver with a certain axe of the value of six pence which she the said Frances in both hands of her the said Frances then and there had and held to, against, and upon the said Charles Silver then and there feloniously wilfully and of her malice aforethought did cast and throw; and that the said Frances Silver with the axe aforesaid so cast and thrown as aforesaid the said Charles Silver in and upon the head of him the said Charles Silver then and there feloniously wilfully and of her malice aforethought did strike & wound giving to the said Charles Silver then and there with the axe aforesaid so as aforesaid by the said Frances Silver cast and thrown in and upon the head of him the said Charles Silver one mortal wound of the length of three inches and of the depth of one inch; of which said mortal wound he the said Charles Silver then and there instantly died; and that the said Blackston Stuart and Barbara Stuart at the time of committing the felony and murder aforesaid by the said Frances Silver in manner and form aforesaid, feloniously wilfully and of their malice aforethought were present aiding helping abetting assisting comforting and maintaining the said Frances Silver in the felony and murder aforesaid in manner and form aforesaid to do commit and perpetrated and so the jurors aforesaid upon the oath aforesaid do say that the said Frances Silver Blackstone Stuart and Barbara Stuart him the said Charles Silver in manner and form aforesaid feloniously wilfully and of their malice aforethought did kill and murder against the peace and dignity of the state

Wm J. Alexander

[On the back, were two sets of numbers and also this: "Record 16 1/2 copy sheets" The witnesses before the grand jury are also listed, along with the jury's verdict: "A true Bill as to Francis Silver Not True Bill as to the others.]

State
vs.
Frances Silver
& others

To Spring term 1832
Gov Pros
Jacob Silver
Margaret Silver
Nancy Wilson
Thomas Silver
John Silver
John Collis
Joseph Tate
——— Howell
Wm Hutchins
David D Baker
Sworn & Seald   B. S. Gaither clk.
[written sideways on back] A true bill as to Francis Silver Not true Bill as to the others

Saml. C. Tate Foreman

Document #3 [two legal pages, written on both sides]

North Carolina   Burke County

Whereas Isaiah Stuart hath complained to us John C. Burgner and Thomas Hughs Two of the acting Justices of the Peace in and for the County of Burke aforesaid that Barbary Stuart, Frankey Silvers & Blackston Stuart have been suspected of having committed a murder on the body of one Charles Silver and whereas it has been made after an oath of the said Isaiah Stuart to us that the said Barbary Stuart, Frankey Silvers & Blackston Stuart have been committed to the Common Goal [jail] of the county aforesaid without the legal forms of trial & without the legal forms of trial and without the parties having it in their power of confronting their accusers before any legal tribunal. There are there fore to command you the Sheriff of Burke County or any other lawfull officer of said County to arrest the bodies of Barbary Stuart, Frankey Silvers and Blackston Stuart and then safely keep so that you have them before us at Morgan within the time Prescribed by Law, then and there to answer the charge & to be further dealt with as the law directs   herein fail not at your Peril Given from under our hands and seal this 13th Day of January A.D. 1832

Thos. Hughes J.P. (seal)
J.C. Burgner J.P. (seal)

[on the same page]

Summon for the state
1 Thomas Howell
2 Wm Hutchins
3 Green Silvers
4 Thomas Silvers
5 Nelly Silvers
6 Nancy Wilson
7 Peggy Silvers
Thomas Howell

Summon for defendant
Wm Hutchins
Jacob Hutchins

[Continuing on the same page]

Isaiah Stuart swears that the above named Barbary Stuart, Franky Silvers and Blackston Stuart, who are now confined in the Common Joal at Morganton for or on a charge of murder were never tried before any legal Tribunal whatever that no witness was examined in the presence of either of the defendants, or in presence of any Magistrate, and that he believes the defendants were committed on the verdict of the Jury of Inquest alone, and without the form of trial as required by law. January 13, 1832

Isaiah (his X mark) Stuart

[next page in different handwriting]

for the plaintiff
X John Sillvers
Green Silvers
X Nancy Willson
X Thomas Silvers
X Nelly Silvers
X Thomas howel
green silver [crossed out]
thomas silver [crossed out]
X William Hutchens
Jacob Hutchen [crossed out]
X Jeames Howel
X Elijah Green
X John Chollis
X Jacob Hutchins
X Joseph Tate

for the Deft.

Issack Grindstaff
Jacob Hutchens
William Hutchens

John Chollis and Joseph Tate each bound in the sum Fifty pounds to appear on the fourth Monday of March Superior Court to give evidence on behalf the State against Franky Silvers and not depart this court without leave this 17 January 1831 [sic]

J.C. Burgner J.P.

State of North Carolina
Burke County
 I Isaiah Stuart acknowledge myself indebted to the State of North Carolina in the sum of one hundred pounds to be levied of my goods and chattels lands and tenements to be void on condition that Barbara Stuart and Blackston Stuart both appear at Morganton on the fourth Monday of March next to give evidence on behalf of the State against Francy Silvers and that they do not depart this court without leave
 This 17 January 1832
Isaiah (his X mark) Stuart

[Next page, folded to from the shuck or outside title for the file.]

State
vs
Barbary Stuart
Franky Silvers
Blackston Stuart

Warrant
1832
Executed as to the
Deft's Inquest
G. Presnell
Witness all sumons
by me C. Baker, Const. [constable]

Defendants Barbary Stuart and Blackston Stuart having Put upon this Trial this day plead not guilty
January 17, 1832

17th January 1832   Warrant delievered before us John C. Burgner and Aron Brittain, Esqr. The Defendants being brought [words repeated and crossed out] before as court Barbara Stuart and Blackston Stuart and an examination of the evidence we are of opinion that the Defendants should be discharged their appearing no evidence on Behalf of the State against them.
A. Brittain J.P.
J.C. Burgner J.P.

Charles Baker as a civil officer is registered to summon all the individuals who may be considered necessary to give evidence in the case of Mrs. Silvers bothe in behalf of the State and the defendant to appear in Morganton on the 17th day of this Inst.
January 13, 1832
John C. Burgner J.P.

Supreme Court Documents

[Note: The following documents from the Supreme Court files in the North Carolina Archives are copied directly from the file made by the young clerk of court in Burke County, Burgess S. Gaither.]

State of North Carolina   Superior Court of Law
Burke County

Be it remembered that at a Superior Court of Law opened and held for the County of Burke in the State of North Carolina at the Court House in Morganton on the fourth Monday of March A.D. 1832 before the honorable John R. Donnell Esquire, one of the judges of the several Superior Courts of Law of said state. The following Grand Jury was drawn from and charged, towit Samuel C. Tate (appointed foreman), Archibald Berry, William Wakefield, William Coffey, Joseph Scott, William Wacker, Rukets Stanly, James Bergin, Bryant Gibbs, James McCall, William Gragg, David Glass, William I. Tate, Thomas Morrison, Isaac Hicks, George Corpening, George Holloway, Jesse R. Hyatt. Who returned into open court a Bill of Indictment in the words and figures Viz.

State of North Carolina   Superior Court of Law
Burke County   Spring Term 1832

The jurors for the state upon their oath present that Frances Silver, Blackston Stuart and Barbara Stuart all of said county not having the fear of God before their eyes, but being moved and seduced by the instigation of the Devil on the twenty second day of December in the year of our Lord one thousand eight hundred and thirty one, with force and arms in the county of Burke aforesaid in and upon one Charles Silver in the peace of God and of the State then and there being feloniously willfully and of true malice aforethought did make an assault, and that the said Frances Silver with a certain axe of the value of six pence which she the said Frances Silver in both the hands of her the said Frances then & there had and held to against and upon the said Charles Silver then and there feloniously willfully and of her malice aforethought did cast and through [throw], and that the said Frances Silver with the axe aforesaid so cast and thrown as aforesaid the said Charles Silver in and upon the head of him the said Charles Silver with the axe aforesaid so cast and thrown as aforesaid the said Charles Silver in and upon the head of him the said Charles Silver then and there feloniously willfully and of her malice aforethought and strike and wound giving to the said Charles Silver then and there with the axe aforesaid so as aforesaid by the said Frances Silver cast and thrown in and upon the head of him the said Charles Silver one mortal wound o fhte length of three inches and of the depth of one inch, of which said mortal wound he the said Charles Silver then and there instantly died and that the said Blackston Stuart and Barbary Stuart at the time of committing the felony and Murder aforesaid by the said Frances Silver in a manner and form aforesaid feloniously willfully and of true malice aforethought were present aiding, helping abetting assisting comforting and maintaining the said Frances Siler in the felony and murder aforesaid in manner and form aforesaid upon the oath aforesaid do say that the said Frances Silver, Blackston Stuart and Barbara Stuart him the said Charles Silver in manner and form aforesaid feloniously willfully and of true malic aforethought did kill and murder agains the peace and dignity of the state—

Wm J. Alexander Sol

On which are the following endorsements, State Vs. Frances Silver and others. Indictment Murder to Spring Term 1832. Gov. Pros. Jacob Silver, Margaret Silver, Nancy Wilson, Thomas Silver, John Silver, John Collis, Joseph Tate, Thomas Howell, William Hutchins, David D. Baker. Sworn and inst. B S Gaither clk: A true Bill as to Frances Silver, not a true bill as to the tohers. Saml C. Tate Foreman—

The Prisoner Frances Silver being brought to the bar was arraigned and on her arraignment plead not guilty on which issue was taken and put herself for her trial upon God and her country. The following persons were tendered accepted and sworn as jurors to pass upon the life and death of the Prisoner at the bar Frances Silver to wit: Henry Pain, Robert McElrath, David Beedle, Oscar Willis, Cyrus P. Connelly, John Hall, William L. Baird, Richard Bean, Joseph Tipps, Lafayette Collins, Robert Garrison, David Hunsaker.

Who after hearing the evidence—argument of council and charge of the Court retired and returned into Court and rendered the following verdict: We find the Prisoner Frances Silver guilty of the felony and murder whereof she stands charged in manner and form as charged in the Bill of Indictment.

Whereupon the Prisoner's council moved for a new trial which rule was granted and after argument ordered to be discharged and the prisoner being at the bar the court passed the following sentence: That the Prisoner Frances Silver be taken back to the prison from whence she came and from there to the place of public execution on the Fayday of Burke July County Court next by the Sheriff of Burke County and then and there to be hung by the neck untill she be dead. From which instance the Prisoner prays and appeal to the Supreme Court and gives for security Isaiah Stuart and Jackson Stuart.

Case: State Vs. Frances Silver
The Prisoner was indicted for the murder of her Husband

The case was one of circumstantial evidence. The witnesses for the state were sworn and separated under the charge of an officer until each was called into court to be examined.

The case was taken up for trial on Thursday morning and occupied the day in the examining of testimony, the argument of council and the charge of the court. The Jury having retired from the Bar under the charge of officers about candle light. The Jury were kept together in deliberations during the night and on the next day returned to the Bar and was called over they stated that they had not yet agreed and expressed a wish to hear some of the witnesses who had been examined again brought into Court that they might be satisfied about their testimony. The court directed the witnesses wanted to be again called in and requested the Jury to ask the questions on such points as they wished to be satisfied about. The Jurors asked the questions and on some points the witnesses went more into detail than they had done on their first examination. The Prisoner's Counsel remarked that the witnesses had been separated during the trial but had come to the bar and had been at large during the night and the court stated to the jury that such was the case that it could not have been anticipated that they would wish to hear any of the witnesses examined again after the case had been put to them and they had returned from the Bar But that this jury ought to hear the witnesses with all the prejudice arising from the circumstances of their having had an opportunity of being together since their former examination. The jury returned a verdict of guilty. The Prisoner's counsel obtained a rule to show cause why a new trial should not be granted on the ground that the witnesses had been permitted to be examined by the jury on the second day when the witnesses had had an opportunity of being together after their first examination. Rule discharged and Judgment of Death. Appealed to the Supreme Court.

J R Donnell

I Burgess S. Gaither, Clerk of Burke County Superior Court of Law in the state of North Caorlina do hereby certify that the foregoing is truly copied from the Records of said Court of the proceedings had in the prosecution The State vs. Frances Silver

[Seal} In Testimony whereof I have hereunto set my hand and affixed the seal of said Court at Morganton the 3d Day of May 1832

B.S. Gaither

Justice Thomas Ruffin's Ruling for the Court

The separation of witnesses is adopted in aid of the cross-examination, as a test of the truth of their testimony by its consistency or inconsistency. It is not founded on the idea of keeping the witnesses from intercourse with each other. That would be a vain attempt. The expectation is not to prevent the fabrication of false stories, but by separate cross-examinations to detect them. Testimony altogether false might be imposed upon the court as true, because delivered by two or more, trained to the same tale; or, as most frequently happens, because some indubitable and undisputed truth is mingled with much or material falsehood. The great safeguard against such a delusion consists in cross-examination, in which a prompt succession of acute, pertinent, peremptory, and sifting interrogatories, not anticipated, and for which answers have not been provided, surprises and betrays the impostor. And such a cross-examination is most effectual when the witness cannot, by a knowledge of the statements of his predecessor, make his own conform to them. The thing to be avoided, then, is not that the witnesses should be together, but that they should be examined together. When interrogated separately, all the witnesses, constantly apprehensive of the detection of falsehood, and finding no facts as they occurred, I find, therefore, nothing in the rule of law or the practice which forbids the examination of witnesses who have been together after being sworn, or even once examined. Indeed, it is usual to keep them together in the same room, and after a witness has been examined, to send him back, if there be an expectation that he will be called again. Had the party wished to recall such a witness, there is nothing to preclude him from doing so, at any stage when it would be competent for the party to recall any witness.

But even that is a much stronger case than the present. The order of trials necessarily imposes upon the parties the duty of making out their cases, at certain stages of the proceedings. They must close at some time and after that they cannot be heard again. But it is entirely regular at all times for the witness to correct his own mistake, or to explain his words that have not been correctly understood. No rule can prescribe to the jury the duty of finding a verdict under misapprehension. So, if the jurors do not understand the words or meaning of the witness alike, it is competent and proper for them to ask for explanation, before it is too late to act on it. The judge may indeed give it from his notes; or, preferring a direct appeal to the witness himself, as being the best able to repeat and explain his words, and as being subjected to the ordeal of examination, he may, in his discretion, again place the witness before the jury. When explanations are thus demanded by the judge or jury, they must be considered as asked for the maintenance of truth, and in execcution of justice. There is no apprehension of trick or imposition in such cases, as there would be were the same privilege in the party. If, indeed, the inquiries of the jury sought evidence that was incompetent, or to put the case made by the parties upon new points, the court would undoutedly inform the jury of their impropriety, and interdict them. But here the reexamination was solely to satisfy the jury of the testimony already given, and the greater detail made necessary only to produce that satisfaction. So we must consider it, for the objection is not taken to the subjects of the interrogatories, or the nature of the answers, but only that the witnesses were examined at all after having been together. In that I see nothing against either practice or principle.

PER CURIAM   The Judgment Be Affirmed
Thomas Ruffin

[From the N.C. Reports: Cited: S. v. Noblett, 47 N.C., 425; Morehead v. Brown, 51, N.C.. 371.]

[The following, with later notes, is from the N.C. Supreme Court files in the North Carolina Archives; a copy is also among the original documents in Morganton. The words, "one sheet" are written at the top.]

The State of N. Car.

v.

Frances Silver

It is considered by the court that the judgment of the Superior Court of Law for the county of Burke be affirmed. And it is ordered that the said Superior Court proceed to judgment and sentence of death against the defendant Frances Silver. On motion judgment is granted against Jackson Stuart and Isaiah Stuart, sureties to the appeal, for the costs of this court in this suit incurred.

Certified by
Jno. L. Henderson
Clk.

[Note written below the above, apparently much later]

Hanged from oak tree John Dickson in front yard (in other words, in John Dickson's front yard.) Property of John Dickson was located on Valdese Ave. Somewhere between White Street and Broadoak Hospital.

Letters and Petitions in the Governor's Papers and the Governor's Letterbooks

[Note: There are two sets of papers in the governor's files. Usually, but not in all cases, the documents in the "papers" are the governor's official acts and those in the "letterbooks" are involved with complaints from private citizens. There are 17 different letters and petitions to Governors Montfort Stokes and David Lowry Swain regarding the Frankie Silver case. Among the documents we know to be missing is a second letter from Stokes' son, Hugh Montgomery Stokes, a young lawyer working in Morganton at the time of the trial. The most important missing document, of course, is Gov. Swain's letter to Thomas W. Wilson explaining why he will not pardon Frankie Silver. There is no copy in the governor's papers or letterbooks and nobody has yet been able to find it among the thousands of pages which Swain very carefully saved. Two of the documents are unsigned copies of the petition listed as Document Number 8. Since they are identical in wording, I have not reproduced them here. All of the other documents are listed in chronological order.]

1. **September 6, 1832, letter**
to Gov. Montfort Stokes from Col. David Newland:

Raleigh 6th Sept. 1832

His Excellency
M. Stokes

When I had the pleasure of being in Wilksboro some time in Apl. last the circumstances of Mrs. Silvers killing her husband was named and you was told that a petition would be presented to you for her pardon. The petitition has come to hand for your consideration. At the time alluded to in Wilksboro you named you did [not] now of there ever having been a female executed in N. Carolina & asked if I had to which I answered in the negative. You then said you would be delicately situated & asked my opinion. I answered that if rumors be trew I thought her a fit subject for example. But Sir from various information which I have rec'd since her trial I am induced to believe her gilt has been much exaggerated which you will perceive by the opinion some gentlemen of the Bar who has assigned her petition & was present & also disinterested during her trial. Upon the whole I realy think her a fit subject for executive Clemency.

Yours sincerely,   D. Newland

2. Petition bearing 113 signatures
addressed to Gov. Montfort Stokes, no date:

To his Excellency M. Stokes, Governor of North Carolina

The undersigned citizens of the county of Burke beg leave humble to represent to your excellency that at the Superior Court held for the county of Burke on the 4th Monday in March last one Frances Silver was convicted & sentence of death passed on her for the murder of her husband Charles Silvers. The execution of which sentence was to have taken place on the 27th July Instant from which sentence the said Francis prayed and obtained an appeal to the Supreme Court. Your petitioners are informed the judgment of the Court below has been affirmed. Your petitioners ask of your excellency to pardon the said Franky and that too for the reason following: To Wit: your petitioners have no intention or reason for impuning the motives of the Jury in rendering a Verdict of guilty against the Defendant or of the Court for its judgment for they do not hesitate to say that the defendant had a Patient, fare and unpartial trial. But that the Verdict was founded entirely on circumstantial evidence there is no doubt. That the defendant is young, not exceeding the years 20 or 22 even now, was raised most of the life right in the county of Burke of Low and humble parentage who have ever been incapable of administering either to the mind or body—such comfort as Nature and Childhood may have required. They represent that the defendant has now an infant child which has been refused her sight ever since she has been immured within the walls of a dungeon which took place the first of January last, the alleged time of the Committing of the offense. They further represent that the defendant has suffered greatly in health since her confinement and is now laboring under disease as they are informed and believe. Your petitioners further represent to your excellency that the execution of a poor woman whose very name tis frailty for example's sake is not called for by the Publick or for the good of County. The only inducement on the part of the defendant for the Commission of the alleged offense was that of brutal conduct of the husband toward the wife—as appeared in evidence. Your petitioners do further represent to your excellency that the execution of a poor female for an alleged offense of this character has so seldom occurred within the history of our county whilst it has so frequently happened that husbands have murdered their wives and escaped Punishment that we believe it would reflect indictable disgrace on the Community. We therefore Pray that your excellency will Pleas to Pardon her of the Sentence Passed on her as we do Verily believe her a fit subject for executive Clemency and mercy—Whereas is duty bound will ever pray—

[Note: There were a total of 113 signatures on this petition, however, several of them were impossible to decipher; in some places, I could make out one of the names but not both; in other cases, where I had to guess at the spelling, I have included a question mark to indicate the writing was not clear.]

B.S. Gaither, Th. W. Wilson, J.D. Ferrer [?], J.B. Bouchelle, Saml. McD. Tate, D. Newland, C.J. Chisholar [?], Ed Hooper, Jess Burgin, Philip Johnson, Thomas Brown, J.K. Norton, John (X his mark) Good, John Hennesa, Seth Kincaid, Jno. E. Wooding, Jonathan Duckworth, P. Mull, Garet Garson, Jesse A. Simmons, Angus McLewer—Captain of the Roanoke blues in garrison in North Carolina, John O. [?] Wilson, Jacob Deal, John Allison, Daniel O. [?], Samuel Capehart, Nicholas Whisenhunt, Hambleton Critian [?], John [?], D. Hawkins, [?] Simson, Cornilius Lain, Henry Mull Sen., Robert L. Wooding, Benjamin F. Long, William F. Thomas, James McCoury, William Bell S., Elrod Poteet, John Yancy, L. Roper, Joseph Curtis, J.M. Carson, Jno. Carssnet, Daniel Jarrett, Philip Martin, Henry Garrison, Mantrivecq [?], William Walker, William Brittain, William Hipps, Zenus Sullivan, George Hipps, Thomas H. Bevens, John H. Pearson, Chs. McDowell, [?] Erwin, William Stalcup, Thomas Balleu, Rowlin Duncan, Jessy S. Walton, John Hall Jr., Robert Garrison Jr., John Mitchell, Jacob Schull, J.W. Carson, Jno. McDowell, Joseph McD. Carson "I was a disinterested spectator and thought the verdict doubtful", N.M. Reinhardt, Chs. Carson, J.P. Henderson, J.E. Lewis, P.E. Saunier [?], J.R. Stallcup, Thomas Weedle, Lewis Powell, John Deal, W.V. Culbertson, Robert Garrison, T. Carlton, John Bartley, Thos. Dale, Joseph England, John Pulliam, [?] Mull, [?] Thompson, Collins Duckworth, John McNeley, William N. Jackson, Joseph Scott, John Scott, Nash A. Giles [?], E.M. Tate, R.C. Pearson, W. Alexander, Chas. Bowman, Joseph Parker, L.W. Alexander, Jno. Mcguire jailor, Moses Wiggans, Ransom Wiggans, Richard Bean, Daniel Williams, Nathaniel Givin, Benjamon Newland, Jno. Mulis, J. H. Newland.

[Note on back of petition: "Petition in favor of Frances Silver/Burke/Not acted on/see petitions to Gov. Swain." The name of Thomas Lloyd is also on the back of the entire document, what would have been the title page or shuck after it had been folded.]

3. Petition to Gov. Montfort Stokes, no date:

STATE OF NORTH CAROLINA
To his Excellency Montfort Stokes

Whereas Frances Silver was convicted of the murder of her Husband Charles Silver at the last Superior Court of Law held for the county of Burke and whereas we the undersigned believing that the death of Charles Silver is involved in so much doubt as the body has never been found that we believe that the public justice of the county does not require that the prisoner should be executed in pursuance of the Constance of the Law.

We are cognizant of the fact that she was convicted on Circumstantial evidence alone and that after hearing the evidence as given out of Counsel & charge of the Judge the Jury retired and returned into court nine for acquitting & three for convicting but owing to the re-examination of witnesses in behalf of the state running into a Trane of Circumstances that were not related in the former examination and which the prisoner had not the opportunity of explaining as she had not introduced any testimony on the first examination. She was precluded by the rule adopted by the court—that no new witness should be examined at that stage of the trial nor remarks of counsel heard—

We the undersigned believe that the circumstances which are supposed to have attended this murder are so totally inconsistent with human nature that the greatest exertion of female fortitude could not possible have accomplished the horrid deed.

We are many of us the neighbors of the prisoner and know her to be a woman of good character and have never heard her charged with any offense heretofore. We therefore pray your excellency to Pardon the Prisoner.

Saml. Newland, Jno. Maguire, Ed Hooper, Abe More, Jas. S. Leonard, Ezra [?], Ths. Henline, James Howel of the inquest, Benjamon Willis, Frances Teller, Isaac Grinestaff one of the inquest, Dannel Tulley [indecipherable sentence by his name], Ansell Cook, Lewis Cook, Adam Hoppes, John McNeill, Hector McNeill, Dim McNeill, Daniel Smith, Malcolm McNeill, Joseph

Godfrey, William Ainsworth, J. Ainsworth, [?] J.P. Ridley, James Shephard, Daniel Beck, Hugh Bentley, Cap. William Piercy, David Hopes, Tomas Weeb, William Panner, George Hoppes, David Oaks, William Dale, Nathan Horney [?] lieut, John Sherrill, William C. Gurley, William Gurley.

4. Letter to Gov. Montfort Stokes from David Newland:

Little River
22d Sept. 1832

My dear governor

On my return home from Raleigh I was anxiously hailed believing I had obtained from your excellency a pardon for Francis Silvers. On reporting that you had not yet determined whether you would pardon her or not it seemed to strike some of your friends with considerable surprise. Since my return home I have learned that seven persons who assigned the petition I presented to your excellency were seven of the jury which convicted her. This fact was unknown to me when I had the pleasure of seeing you in Raleigh. The persons who assigned her petition that were jurors is Robt. Garrison, Mr. Macklerath, & five others whose names I do not recollect. But that seven of the names on the petition in your possession were seven of the jurors who found her guilty I feel very confident. From the source I received the information of I have the utmost confidence, I named to Mr. Wilson her Atty. that you required further Remonstrance viz.—a statement from the whole of the jury who condemned her and he Mr. Wilson said he would perceive & send you such petition. But whither he does or not from this additional fact before you I cannot help but believe your good hospitable and friendly feelings together with your good judgment will extend mercy to an humble & penitent Convict. I am my dear governor yours in sincerity.

D Newland

5. Letter to Gov. Montfort Stokes
from his son, Hugh Montgomery Stokes, October 29, 1832:

Wilkes Octo. 29th 1832

My Dear Sir:

Isaiah Stewart, the father of Mrs. Silvers, condemned for the murder of her husband at the March term of Burke Sup. Co. Law, whose petition for her pardon has heretofore been referred to you for the exercise of executive clemency; has been here again to know whether that clemency has been or will be extended to her—

I could not inform him upon that matter, as I have never been able to do so.— The county court of Burke complains of the cost: (a very common complaint to hide the operation of the laws). 'Tis their own fault not to correct the crimes of the country by a rigid enforcement of those dictates which comes within their original and appropriate powers.— However this may be, if a pardon is granted or intimated to be granted, the only course to be pursued, is pleading a prospect of pardon before some one of the circuit judges in open court at Burke Sup. Co. Law next or by write of habeas corpus at this or (some one of their chambers, or to the sheriff under the gallows.— If a pardon has already been granted under the great seal and her father or other friend is willing to incur the expense of a habeas corpus; 'twould then be well for her attorney (Mr. Thos. Wilson) to be apprised thereof (he now resides in Morganton).

What course your own good sense may prompt you to do in this matter, I must necessarily leave with yourself. — I have since writing before been at Burke; the excitement raised against the culprit is rapidly subsiding : and I have but little hesitation in saying it will totally subside before the re-condemnation can be made except with the family and connections of the husband of Mrs. Silvers, whose existence at this time is extremely doubtful.—

I know of but one execution of a white woman since the formation of our present government, though there may have been more.— An execution of this last as well as the crime of which the culprit stands charged is so enormous that natural reason as well as feeling, stands opposed to the execution or commission of either.—

I hope that you may not find it inconsistent with the known [indecipherable word] of your own disposition as well as the known [?] and forebearance of the laws of the country toward the weaker part of creation to grant pardon to the culprit heretofore mentioned—farther than what is contained in my former letter I cannot state—the family are well and have expected you home for some time.

Yours truly,
H.M. Stokes

[NOTE: the "former letter" which Hugh Stokes refers to is not in the governor's papers or the governor's letterbooks.]

6. Letter to Gov. Montfort Stokes
from David Newland, November 3, 1832:

Kerner's X Roads
3d Nov. 1832

My dear governor

You will receive in company with this a line from your Son relating to the petition in favor of Mrs. Silvers of Burke Co. The Stage Horn is now Blowing for a start & I am obliged to go. I can only say Pardon her if you can & send her pardon to Tho. Wilson.

Yours in grate haste
D. Newland

7. Letter to Gov. Montfort Stokes from Thomas W. Wilson, Frankie Silver's attorney, November 19, 1832:

[Note: The frequent dashes do not mean that words have been deleted from Wilson's letters; they are Wilson's own method of punctuation.]

Statesville   19 November 1832

My dear Sir

I hope you will Pardon my troubling you with these few lines. The importance of the subject I wish to mention will plead my Justification. It is the condition of the unfortunate Lady who is now confined in our jail in Morganton Franky Silvers. She has been induced fore some little time to believe a pardon had been granted by your excellency. This opinion got abroad through a misunderstanding of Col. David Newland. It is not ncecessary that I should multiply words or reasons why I think she should win a pardon. Suffer it to say that I have no hesitation in saying that the community expect her a pardon & I believe generally wish it—— Mr. Joseph Carson was present at the trial to whom I refer you He I know at one time he thought it a case very doubt-ful I saw David Newland at Wilksboro & rec'd the letter which Hugh M. Stokes wrote on that subject. I fully concur in sentiment with him as to the opinion of the community. There certainly are but few now who think or wish her execution. It is believed by many that her parents were very instrumental in the perpetration of that horrid deed. If so, surely it is a powerful reason why the executive clemency should be extended to one of her age and condition. I know my dear sir that you have often been reproached for extending the Pardon's Power...[unclear word] in the execution. You have nothing to fear in this reproach. Human-ity is certainly one of the greatest attributes. I do hope and trust Sir that if it is consistent with your duty & feelings towards a poor miserable retch that you will gant her a pardon (if not already done) and forward the same to me at Morganton. I did request Mr. Boon our sheriff to speak to you on the Subject. I know your engagement and fear that I have already worn your patience. Please to accept the assurances of my highest esteem and regard for your Duties

Tho. W. Wilson

8. Petition to Gov. David Lowry Swain from Frances Silver through her lawyer, Thomas W. Wilson, dated June 3, 1833.

[Note: nothing has been deleted from this document; the dashes are Wilson's own. There are 3 copies—identical in wording, but in different handwriting—of the following petition in Vol. 47, Governor's Papers, pages 207, 209, and 211; a fourth copy is located on page 227; it is signed by Thos. Wilson and Samuel Hillman. On the back of this one is the following notation: "Respited to the 2d Friday in July 1833 Rejected finally."]

to his Excellency David L. Swain
Governor of the State of North Carolina

The petition of Francis Silvers of the county of Burke respectfully represents to your Excellency that at March term 1832 of the Superior Court of Burke she was convicted of the Crime of having murdered her husband Charles Silvers, a crime of the deepest dye and which was aggravated by every circumstance which could give a darker colouring to the transaction and to your petitioner the most fiend like disposition—

Your immediate predecessor and your excellency have been petitioned for a pardon for your petitioner.

The facts set forth in the petitions were only garbled statements of what transpired upon the trial—The evidence against your petitioner was entirely circumstantial—NO one knows but your petitioner the circumstances and the truth of the facts under which the act was committed—Being a woman and entirely ignorant of the laws of the country she felt a repugnance to making any confession from a fear of involving herself in still greater difficulties—until the decision of the Supreme Court confirming the decision of the Superior Court of Burke and until sentence of death was a second time passed upon her and the day of execution appointed she had hopes that her life would still be spared—Nor were her hopes then entirely extinguished—Escape was then her only hope—That she effected by what means she will never disclose—She was retaken and again incarcerated—From that moment she lost all hope—Under the impending responsibility of passing from time into eternity she made a free and full disclosure of all the facts and circumstances attending this unhappy occurrence, not doubting but what it would in the estimation of the world greatly aggravate her guilt and forever consign her character to disgrace and infamy—To her great surprise she found that many respectable and intelligent gentlemen who had before kept aloof, stepped forward and said if her confession were true, she ought not to be executed—Your petitioner avers that the confession made in the presence of William C. Bevens and Thomas Wilson Sheriff is true in every particular and whatever may be her fate, she believes that it has been submitted to scrutiny which will convince the world that is is true—Under these impressions and by the advice of others your petitioner is emboldened again as to ask of your excellency that executive clemency which it is your power to bestow, to extend to your petitioner a pardon a pardon [sic] for the crime of which she has been convicted and save to North Carolina the disgrace of seeing a woman under the gallows.

The undersigned having seen a statement of the Confession of Francis Silvers and been requested to sign a petition for a pardon were or at least a part of us induced to think that the statement might have received a colouring from the individual who wrote it and by possibility that words might have been put in her mouth calculated to elicit the answers which she gave—For the purpose of satisfying ourselves we repaired to the Jail heard her statement in her own language, carried her through a cross-examination and the result was a conviction upon our minds that the statement made in the presence of William C. Bevens and Thos. Wilson DS [deputy sheriff] is substantially true —

June 3d, 1833
Th. W. Wilson

[On the same page as the above]

The Undersigned citizens of Burke having seen the confession of Francis Silver and the statement of the gentlemen who examined her touching the same believe that she is a suitable subject for executive clemency to extend to her a pardon for the crime of which she has been convicted
June 3d 1833

Ja. T. Downey
Calvin C. Pows
John Adams
D.W. Thomas
J. Robards
Wm Craig

Samuel G. Wooton
Robert S. Wooding
Nathan Smalley
J. Stickney
Oscar Willis, a Juror
John McElrath

9. Petition to Gov. David L. Swain, dated June 3, 1833 in which wording is identical to that of No. 8.

The undersigned citizens of Burke having seen the Confession of Francis Silver and the statements of the Gentlemen who examined her touching the same believe she is a suitable object for executive clemency and respectfully ask of your excellency to extend to her a pardon for the crime of which she has been conficted.

June 3d 1833

James Howell
John Gofreys P
Leonard M. Gurly
Alford Hollands
William Gurley
William Stafford
Thos Young
Thomas McTaggart

JW Carson

William Seagley

10. Petition to Gov. David L. Swain, dated June 3, 1833, in which the wording is identical to that of No. 8:

The undersigned citizens of Burke County Having seen the confession of Frances Silvers and the statement of the Gentlemen who examined her touching the same believe that she is a suitable object for executive clemency and respectfully ask of your excellency to extend to her a pardon for the crime of which she has been convicted.

June 3d 1833

Wm Stallings	Jesse Conley
John Sherrill	Hugh Conley
John Young (Yancy)	Wm B. Rust
Thomas Walker	Joseph England
Randall Dugald	John P. Wood
Wm. Washburn	Allen Griffin
Jesse R. Stallcup	G Hawkins
Eli Robins	George Ward
William Reed	Wm Griffin
Washington Beach	[illegible name]
George S. Walton	Killian Jarrett
Jesse S. Hattan	Daniel M. Galliard
William England	

11. Letter to Gov. David L. Swain from William F. Thomas, dated June 3, 1823:

Brindletown   June 3d 1833

His excellency David L. Swain
Sir
You have been petitioned for to pardon of Mrs. Sylvers who has been condemned to death for the murder of her husband

and is now living under your respite. I did not sign the petition for her pardon believing her unworthy of Executive Clemency and seeing the public would not be satisfied with her pardon. But now I will assure you that public opinion is entirely changed & I am under the impression that nine tenth of the inhabitants of Burke County would cheerfully sign a petition & would rejoice at her pardon.

That public indignation which at one time was so strong appears to be satisfyed & now the belief is prevalent that she killed him in a fracous, that part of her confession is not doubted though the manner in which she disposed of him is not fully believed. I saw Gov. Burton who told me he had a conversation with you on the subject but at the time he left Burke the community was under great excitement   therefore he was not able to draw a rational reference what would be the sentiments after that fever subsided.

It was from the result of the conversation with Gov Burton that I have been induced to write you not having an opertunity to see him in time as the thread of her existence is but short I would have requested him to have written you on the subject. Several others who I have spoken to on the subject would write but they believe the time too short for you to receive & answer before the day of Execution.

The subject who has been praying your clemency I have never seen but once. Know nothing of her nor her family untill Since she committed the act; but I do believe the public is satisfied & that no good would result from the example of her execution.

These things I set forth without speaking to or being requested by an individual of her relations. I am unknown personally to you as I never saw you except at J.E. Patton's near Brindletown. When Inside I am doing business in company with him.

If you cannot consistent with the duties of your office pardon her I would merely suggest to you that if you could consistently extend her respite. If you think proper to act on this mater you would have thru by sending on an express who would reach here before her execution. I am respectfully

Yours
Wm F Thomas

12. Letter to Gov. David L. Swain from Thomas W. Wilson, dated June 12, 1833:

Morganton   Jun 12th 1833

To His Ecly David L. Swain
Govr. of the State of N.C.
                                        Morganton, June 30th 1833

    You will be somewhat surprised at seeing this petition and letter after our makeing on your part a peremptory refusal to pardon without a different [illegible word] on the [illegible word] of the affair could be produced. Mr. Stuard the father of the prisoner was advised by Col. John Carson as being a means by which he might possibly obtain a pardon together with others of the village to get up a petition among the ladies. The prisoner however knows nothing of it but is preparing for Death to this proceeding however I have not advised either for or against. The minds of the People seem to be very much softened in her behalf since the determination on your Behalf with regard to a pardon. I am requested by Mr. Stuard to ask your excellency to add an addition to her respite. He thinks he will be able to add new light on the subject and the people think if there are any ground upon which to add to time it might possible aid in the cause of Justice and Humanity.

                    Respectfully,
                    Your Obt. Sert.
                    WC Bevins

15. Letter from Gov. David L. Swain to W.C. Bevins, dated July 9, 1833:

Dear Sir

I have received your letter without date [Note: the letter from Bevins was clearly dated June 30, 1833; Swain was apparently trying to say he did not get the letter in time to save Frankie from execution on July 12, 1833] but post marked on the 3rd inst. together with the accompanying petition of a number of the most respectable Ladies of your Vicinity in behalf of the unfortunate Mrs. Silvers, who before this communication can reach you, will in all human probability have passed the boundary which separates us alike from the reproaches of enemies and the sympathies of friends. All that is now in my power to do is to Unite in the anxious wish which doubtless pervades the whole community to which she belongs, that she may find that mercy in Heaven which seemed to be necessarily denied upon earth, a free pardon for all the offenses in her life.

I beg you to assure the fair petitioners, with the most of whom I have the pleasure of an acquaintance that the benevolent motives which influenced their memorial in behalf of the unfortunate convict, are duly appreciated and that no one can participate more deply than I do in their sympathy for her melancholy fate.—

I am, Sir, very respectfully
Your Obt. Servt.
D.L. Swain

More on the Stewart Family

Most of the following is from a genealogy entitled, *Stewart Line*, published by Dan W. Olds, 313 Pinelake Court, Spartanburg, S.C., dated March 10, 1997.

William Stewart left a will in Anson County, N.C., dated November 25, 1816, which was probated in January of 1817. In the will, William Stewart named his wife, Priscilla, and the following children: Joseph Stewart, John Stewart, Isaiah Stewart, William Stewart, Phebe Stewart, Delilah Stewart, Frances Stewart, Mary Stewart. Isaiah Stewart was a witness when William Stewart, planter, sold 150 acres to William Jenkins; William Stewart had been granted the land on March 9, 1799. If the above Isaiah Stewart was the father of Frances who married Charles Silver [and was, thus, named for her aunt], then the line continues as follows. The 1820 census of Anson County lists the families of Murdoch, William and Isaiah Stewart, all living south of Richardson's Creek. Isaiah Stewart's household included two males under 10 [Joseph and Blackstone?], one male 10-15 [Jackson], one male between 16 and 18, two males 16-25; one male over 44; one female under 10 [Frances?] and one female 26-44.

This Isaiah Stewart sold 175 acres in Anson County, adjoining Jackson Stewart's, on March 18, 1823, to Charles Stewart. He sold 155 acres to William Stewart November 15, 1825 and apparently took his family to the mountains. On August 30, 1830, "Ice" Stewart and Zachariah Candler were witnesses to a deed in Buncombe County from Charles Stewart to Nathan Stewart. [This land was in what would become Yancey County.] Isaiah Stewart's name does not appear in grantor or grantee indexes in Buncombe or Yancey Counties. The 1830 census for Burke County lists the family of Isaiah Steward. He and his wife were listed under the column 40-50; with 1 male 10-15, 2 females 15-20. [Olds notes that Isaiah and Barbara should have been ten years older than this.]

Isaiah Stewart married Barbara _____. She was 72 in the 1850 census and so born about 1778. She listed her birthplace as Virginia. There are no documents as to her name before marriage. The following list of children was obtained by Olds from Chandler Stewart, a descendant of Joseph Stewart, born 1813, who said his father's Bible had a list of the brothers— John, Jackson, Joseph, and Blackstone.

Children of Isaiah and Barbara Stewart:

1. John C. Stewart was born March 9, 1800 [?] and died February 22, 1893. He married Mahala Gurley. She was born June 15, 1810 and died June 15, 1909.

2. Jackson Stewart was born August 18, 1807 and died November 12, 1864. He married Elizabeth Howell, who lived from 1808 to 1888. Children of Jackson and Elizabeth Howell Stewart:

A. William Robert Stewart was born February 23, 1828 and died December 23, 1896. His will dated March 20, 1896 probated in Mitchell County. He married Lockey _____.

B. Mary Stewart was born August 27, 1829; she married Sam Sparks.

C. Susan Stewart was born September 18, 1831 and died in March of 1887. Listed as Susannah in the census. She married Tom Greene.

D. Isabella Stewart was born May 7, 1833 and died about 1915. She first married John Greene [1830-1863]; and then married Joseph Stewart on January 20, 1866, according to Mitchell County marriage records. The 1880 census lists her with Joseph Stewart, age 45, and with Greene and Stewart children. Her tombstone at Bear Creek says, "Isabell Stewart, 1834-1916."

E. Nancy Stewart was born November 9, 1837 and died July 22, 1922. She married John Fortner who was born December 25, 1832 and died April 1, 1900. These dates are from their tombstones in their private cemetery in Mitchell County.

F. Charles D. Stewart was born April 17, 1840 and died February 6, 1914. He married Mary Ann Burleson on September 17, 1865.

G. Jasper Stewart was born April 17, 1843 and died June 22, 1864, killed in the Civil War.

H. Isaac Stewart was born February 4, 1846 and died April 26, 1887. He fought in the Civil War, although only 17. He married Martha Burleson in Mitchell County on May 3, 1863.

I. Cester E. Stewart was born October 23, 1850. Her death certificate says she was born October 23, 1845 [9?] and died June 30, 1927. According to Lloyd Bailey and census records, Cester was short for Jocester and she married "Lace" Byrd, Lace being short for Lazarus. They are listed as Lazarus and Jocester in the 1870 census, ages 32 and 19; and in the 1880 census as Lace and Cester, ages 40 and 29.

J. James M. Stewart was born March 3, 1852. [There is some confusion as to name—called Richard or Dick by some—and his death dates.]

3. Joseph Stewart was born December 12, 1813 and died March 31, 1863. He married Elizabeth Gibbs Finley. Their son, Joseph S. Stewart, was the grandfather of Chandler Stewart.

4. Blackstone Stewart was born in 1817. He and his wife were 20-30 in the 1840 Yancey County census. In the 1850 census, he lists his age as 33, and his property value at $200. His mother, Barbary Stewart, is living in his household at the time of the 1850 census. Blackstone Steward or Stewart does not appear in the 1860 census. [Was he hanged for horse theft in Kentucky, as the legend has it?] According to the census, he married Levina, age 33 in 1850, and they had the following children:

A. Berry, 10

B. Joseph, 7

C. Louisa E., 12

5. Frances Stewart was born around 1810 and married Charles Silver around 1830. Charles died December 22, 1831; Frankie was hanged July 12, 1833. They had one child:

A. Nancy Silver was born November 3, 1830. [For more detailed information on Nancy Silver and her descendants, see the chapter headed "Frankie's Child."]

6. Jacob Stewart is listed as a possible son by Chandler Stewart; a Jacob Stewart is listed in the 1830 Buncombe Census as between 50-60 years old; he would be too old to be a brother of Frankie. Also, the late Lawrence Wood heard stories about a Jacob Stewart who settled in Macon County. According to Wood, the Stewarts in Macon county were definitely related to Frankie and that was the reason her daughter ended up living and dying out there.

7. Charles Stewart. A Charles Stewart is listed as 20-30 in the 1830 Burke census and also in Burke in 1840 as between 40-50. He is also listed in estate records of Isaiah Stewart.

1850 census records on Stuarts/Stewarts/Stewards

1850 Yancey
page 409 Stewart, Jackson, 43, property valued at $2,800
William R., 22,
Charles, 11,
Jackson, 7,
Isaac, 5
Elizabeth, 42,
Mary, 19,
Susannah, 17
Elizabeth, 16
Nancy, 13
Chester, 4½
John Green, 20, laborer

page 429 Steward, Blackstone, 33, farmer property worth $200

Berry, 10
Joseph, 7
Levinia, 33
Louisa E., 12
Barbary, 72, born in Virginia

Estate Records of Isaiah Stuart from the N.C. Archives
[printed document with names and dates written in]

State of North Carolina
Burke County

Know all men by these presents, that we Barbara Stuart, Charles Stuart and Joseph Stuart are held and firmly bound unto the state of North Carolina, for the time being, in the sum of three hundred dollars, current money, to be paid to the said state; To the which payment well and truly to be made, we bind ourselves, our heirs, executors, and administrators, jointly and severally, firmly by these presents. Sealed with our seals, and dated this 25 day of April Anno Domini 1836.

The condition of this obligation is such, that if the above bounded Barbara Stuart administrator of all and singular the goods and chattels, rights and credits of Isaiah Stuart deceased, do make or cause to be made, a true and perfect inventory of all and singular the goods and chattels, rights and credits of the deceased, which have or shall come to the hands, knowledge or possession of the said Barbara Stuart or into the hands or possession of any person for h——; [sic] and the same so made, do exhibit, or cause to be exhibited into Burke County Court, within the time prescribed by law, after the date of these presents: And the same goods, chattels and credits, and all other the goods, chattels and credits of the deceased at the time of his death, or which at any time hereafter shall come into the hands or possession of the said Barbara Stuart or into the hands or possession of any other person or persons for her do well and truly administer according to law; and further do make or cause to be made a true and just account of her said administration, agreeable to law, after the date of these presents: and all the rest and residue of the said goods, chattels, and credits, which shall be found remaining upon the said administratrix account (the same being first allowed by the Governor and Council, Superior or County Court) shall deliver and unto such person or persons respectively as the same shall become due, pursuant to the true intent and meaning of the act in that case made and provided. And if it shall appear that any Will or Testament was made by the deceased, and the executor or executors therein named do exhibit the same in Court, making request to have it allowed and approved accordingly, if the said Barbara Stuart above bounden, being thereunto required, do render and deliver the said letters of administration, (approbation of such Testament being first had and made in the said Court) then this obligation to be void, otherwise to remain in full force and virtue.

Signed, sealed and delivered in the presence of

J.J. Erwin Clk   Barbara (her mark) X Stuart
                          Joseph (his mark)X Stuart
                          Charles Stuart

Note on back of the above: Admr. Bond   Isaiah Stuart estate; 1833 crossed out and 1836 written across..

[handwritten]
    State of North Carolina   Court of Pleas & C
    Burke County   April term 1836

Ordered by Court that William B. Rust as a Justice of the Peace and Joshua Gibbs   Jesse Hyatt and John Rutherford as freeholders be commissioners to lay off and allot unto Barbara Stuart widow and relict of Isaiah Stuart her years allowance out of the crop stock and provision on hand for the support of herself and family for one year and report the same under their hands and seals to next court

Test J.J. Erwin clk

We the undersigned commissioners appointed by this worshipful county court of Burke county at their April Session 1836 to lay off and allot to Barbara Stewart widow & relict of Isaiah Stewart decd one years provisions have this day met and after being duly sworn have laid off and allotted the following articles.

To Wit.

1 Roan mare	20 lbs. sugar
1 cow & calf	10 lbs coffee
1 Hog	2 bushels salt
100 bushels corn	100 lbs flour
300 lbs. bacon	

Of the above articles the Roan Mare, 1 cow & calf, 1 Hog & 25 lbs bacon is all that is shown to us—

We therefore allow as an equivalent, the sum of Eighty five Dollars in cash out of the sale of the Estate when made. Given under our hands & seals this 23rd day of May 1836.

Jno Rutherford jnr
Jesse R. Hyatt
Joshua Gibbs

[written on back of above] Order to William R. Rust; Commisrs. Allowance/1 years Provision for Barbara Stewart

[handwritten]

North Carolina	Court of Pleas and Quarter Sessions
Burke County	Spring Term 1836

To the worshipful county court of the county aforesaid Barbary Stuart v. [or on] the personal estate of Isaiah Stuart deceased petition herewith to your worship that Isaiah Stuart deceased some time in February past, that she is his widdow & Relick that by law she is entitled to one years allowance out of the ——— ——— [two words] & Provisions of the Estate of said Stuart, she therefore prays that your worship will designate and appoint a Justice of the Peace & three freeholders to allot & lay off the same for your petitioner and she in duty bound will ever pray

Th. W. Wilson
attorney for petitioner

[written on back]
Barbary Stewart v. Personal Estate of I. Stewart
Petition April term 1836

Wm. Rust Esqr.
Joshua Gibbs
Jesse Hyatt
John Rutherford

April 26th 1836

Inventory of the property of Isaiah Steuard Decd. Given in by the administrator Barbarah Steuard the wife which was legally appointed by the Court April term 1836.

Viz

1 = Mare
1 = Cow & Calf
2 = Feather Beds & Furniture
2 = Dutch ovens with Lids
1 = Skillet
2 = Shovel ploughs with Stocks
2 = Single Trees & Clevises
2 = Weeding hoes
1 = pr. hames & —auring Chains
2 = Bed Steds
1 = Large Chest
1 = Pewter dish
1/2 dozen pewter plates
2 = pewter Basons
1 = tin pot
1 = Foot Wheel
1 = Grindstone
2 = Iron wedges
1 = handsaw
2 = Augers
1 = Drawing knife
1 = Hog 1- water pail 1- piggin

1 = small calf hide
1 = small piece upper leather & some sole leather
1 = Falling Ax
1 = Mattock
1 = Small Tub
1 = Reap Hook
3 = Small B—ls
1 = Fire Shovel
3 = Sitting Chairs
1 = Small Chair
2 = pr. pot hooks
23 = Washing Spools
3 = Earthen Boals

The following is the amount of sales of said decd. estate Amt $86.87

Barbara X (her mark) Stuart Admr.

Sworn to in open court
July 23, 1836

J.J. Erwin Clk

[written on back]
inventory of the Property of Isaiah Steuard Decd. Given in By Barbarah Steuard Administrator   Recorded 1836

More on Frankie's Child

At the April, 1836, Court of Common Pleas and Quarter Sessions of Burke County, with justices James Avery, R.C. Pearson, and John Collett, the following was ordered:

"Ordered by the court that Nancy Silver, an orphan daughter of Francis Silver, deceased, being about five years old the 3rd day of November, 1835, be bound unto Barbara Stuart until she is eighteen years of age; to receive at her freedom one cow and calf, two suits of clothes, one good bed and furniture and twelve months schooling."

If Nancy was five years old on that date, then she was born November 3, 1830 and so would have been a year and six weeks old at the time of the murder.

In the 1850 census, Barbara Stuart is living with her son Blackstone, but her granddaughter Nancy is not listed in that household.

According to Buck Bryant's account in the *Charlotte Observer*, Nancy Silver married David Parker and he was killed at First Manassas. He also says she has remarried and was reported to be living in Madison County at that time, 1903. There must be some Madison connection because several other accounts also mention it.

The 1860 Yancey County census has the following in Ledger Township: David Parker, 32, farmer [real and personal property] $250, $257, he and all others were born in N.C. as were their parents.

Nancy, 29,

Jacob, 7

Charles W., 5

Phinetter E., 3,

Margaret A., 1, [Margaret Alice]
The Parkers lived next door to Green B. Silver, real and personal property each valued at $10,000; age 64, born in Maryland. He would have been Nancy's great-uncle, the brother of her father's father, Jacob Silver.
Others in Silver household:
Malinda, 41,
Lodima E., 17
Margaret M., 14
George W., 14
John P. , 5
Alexander B., 2
William Thomas, 20, farm laborer

In Volume XIII of *North Carolina Troops, 1861-1865*, published 1993 by the N.C. Archives, is the following under Company B, 54th Regiment, made up largely of men from the Yancey-Mitchell-McDowell area:

> PARKER, DAVID, Private: Born in Mcdowell County and was by occupation a farmer prior to enlisting in Yancey County on March 21, 1862. Reported present or accounted for through October, 1863. Captured at Rappahannock Station, Virginia, November 7, 1863. Confined at Point Lookout, Maryland, November 11, 1863. Paroled at Point Lookout on or about March 9, 1864. Received at City Point, Virginia, March 15, 1864, for exchange. Returned to duty on an unspecified date. Wounded in the forearm at New Market [?] (sic) Virginia, September 24, 1864. Hospitalized at Charlottesville, Virginia.Transferred to Lynchburg, Virginia, September 27, 1864. Returned to duty on an unspecified date. Hospitalized in Richmond, Virginia, March 28, 1865, with a gunshot wound of the right thigh. Place and date wounded not reported. Captured in hospital at Richmond on April 3, 1865. Died in hospital at Richmond on April 14, 1865, of wounds.

Frankie's Grandchildren

According to her tombstone, Nancy Silver Parker was born November 3, 1830 and died September 30, 1901. David Parker was born in McDowell County. He married Nancy Silver on October 20, 1850, according to James D. Silver of 64 South Fairfield Drive, Dover, DE 19901. David Parker was the son of William and Mary Epply Parker; she was the daughter of Peter and Susannah Schrum Epply. According to Lawrence Wood, she was married the second time to William C. Robinson, in Macon County on January 10, 1872. They had one son named Commodore Robinson. Her tombstone bears her first husband's surname. She is buried in the Mount Grove cemetery in Macon County.

One of her descendants, Robert Buchanan of Asheville, says that Nancy was listed in the 1850 census as Jane Silver in the household of William Roberson. Buchanan also says that after she married David Parker and he went off to war, the family was devastated by raiders from all sides. He recalls a family tradition that one of Nancy's sons took their last cow off to sell it and was never seen again; this could be confused with the later story of Charles Westley Parker leaving his family in Macon County.

The following dates were provided by Lawrence Wood of Franklin, N.C. Nancy Silver Parker was born November 3, 1830 and died in Macon County, N.C., September 30, 1901. Children of David and Nancy Silver Parker: 1. Jacob William Parker; 2. Charles Westley Parker; 3. Netter Elizabeth Parker; 4. Margaret Alice Parker; 5. Magdalina Mariah Parker; 6. Cansada Parker.

I. **Jacob William Parker** was born September 7, 1852. He married Lucetta Moses.

II. **Charles Westley Parker** was born September 13, 1854. He married Malissa Moses.

III. **Phinetter or Netter Elizabeth Parker** was born April 27, 1857. She married a Barrett from Union County, Ga.

IV. **Margaret Alice Parker** was born February 1, 1859. She married John Henry Makamey Thomas.

V. **Magdalina Mariah Parker** was born March 1, 1861. She married William T. Gregory.

VI. **Cansada (Kansas) Parker** was born July 29, 1865 and died December 13, 1894. She married Jesse G. Owens.

Frankie's Great Grandchildren and Their Descendants
I. The descendants of Frankie's grandson, Jacob William Parker:

William, or Bill, Parker as he was called, was born September 7, 1852 and died November 9, 1938. He married Lucetta Moses, daughter of Athen and Minerva Peek Moses. Children of Bill and Lucetta Moses Parker: 1. Jerome Parker; 2. Creed Parker; 3. Sam Parker; 4. Athen Parker; 5. David Parker;

6. Nettie Parker; 7. Buena Vista Parker; 8. Ira Parker.

1. Jerome Parker, born in 1876, married Margaret Pressley and they moved to Colorado.

2. Creed Parker, born in 1879, married Birdell Hedden

3. Samuel Parker, born in May of 1884, married first to Becky Pressley; second to Elizabeth Parker and third to Eleanor Dalton.

4. Athen Parker was born in 1886.

5. David H. Parker married Esther Mae Wilson

6. Nettie Lucretia Parker married Henry Crouch

7. Buena Vista Parker was born June 23, 1873 and died August 31, 1947. She married Leander Young, who was born December 19, 1865 and died December 2, 1925. Children of Leander and Buena Vista Parker Young: A. Lida Young; B. Annie Young; C. Florida Young; D. Inez Young; E. Jack Young; F. Louin Young; G. Luther Young.

F. Louin Young married Lillie Adams. Children of Louin and Lillie Adams Young: a. Lester Ray Young was born April 7, 1934 and married Joyce Greer; b. Clifton Lee Young was born December 4, 1935 and married Stella Henry; c. Wardie Lovale Young was born February 27, 1938 and married Judy C. Price; d. Edna Laverne Young was born June 28, 1940 and married Jim Tippett; e. Doyle Tabner Young was born February 23, 1943 and married Shirley Ann Houston; f. Dewey Dale Young was born April 30, 1946; g. Bonnie Lou Young was born April 22, 1948 and married Earl B. Angel.

a. Lester Ray Young married Joyce Greer. Children of Lester and Joyce Greer Young: 1. Tony Young; 2. Lisa Raye Young.

b. Clifton L. Young married Stella Henry. Children of lifton and Stella Henry Young: 1. Karen Young; 2. Melissa Young.

c. Wardie L. Young married Judy C. Price. Children of Wardie and Judy Price Young: 1. Diedra Young.

d. Edna Laverne Young married Jim Tippett. Child of Jim and Edna Laverne Young Tippett: Kimberly Gail Tippett.

e. Doyle T. Young married Shirley Ann Houston. Child of Doyle and Shirley Houston Young: 1. Rhonda L. Young.

f. Bonnie Lou Young married Earl Bernard Angel. Child of Earl and Bonnie Lou Young Angel: 1. Shannon Angel.

8. Ira Parker married Parker Blackburn, son of Calvin and Matilda Moore Blackburn. Children of Parker and Ira Parker Blackburn: A. Zelma Blackburn married Isaac Passmore; B. Iva Blackburn married Frank Dills;

C. Stella Blackburn married Verge Hooper; D. Howard Blackburn; E. Sallie Blackburn married John Stiwinter; F.. Ida Mae Blackburn married Gus Moss; G. Roy Blackburn.

A. Zelma Blackburn married Isaac Passmore. Children of Isaac and Zelma Blackburn Passmore: a. Evelyn Passmore; b. Woodrow Passmore; c. Vernon Passmore; d. Truman Passmore; e. Gene Passmore; f. Lyn Wood Passmore; g. Rhoda Faye Passmore; h. Floyd Passmore.

B. Iva Blackburn married Frank Dills. Children of Frank and Iva Blackburn Dills: a. Ethel Dills.

a. Ethel Dills married Bob Taylor. Children of Bob and Ethel Dills Taylor: 1. Wade Taylor; 2. Wayne Taylor; 3. Frank Taylor; 4. Linda Taylor; 5. Carol Ann Taylor.

C. Stella Blackburn married Verge Hooper. Child of Verge and Stella Blackburn Hooper: a. Griffon Hooper.

D. Sallie Blackburn married John Stiwinter. Children of John and Sallie Blackburn Stiwinter: a. Patsy Stiwinter; b. Randall Stiwinter; c. Sandra Stiwinter.

E. Ida Mae Blackburn married Leamon Norris. Children of Leamon and Ida Mae Blackburn Norris: a. Calvin Norris; b. Keith Norris; c. Kascen Norris.

F. Bertha Blackburn married Gus Moss. Children of Gus and Bertha Blackburn Moss: a. Joyce Carolyn Moss was born January 18, 1947 and married Bobby Smith; b. Leland Moss was born August 4, 1942; c. Glenda Moss was born April 3, 1949 and married Marvin Bryson.

II. The descendants of Frankie's grandson, Charles Parker.

Charles Westley Parker was born September 13, 1854. He married Malissa Moses, daughter of Athen and Mary Minerva Peek Moses. She was born September 21, 1855. Lawrence Wood said he remembered hearing one of Charles' children tell about seeing his or her daddy riding off on a mule. He never came back to his very large family. And, in the 1900 census, Malicy A. Parker is listed as head of the household. She told the census taker she had given birth to 11 children and 10 were still living. Nine of her children are listed in the census: A. Isabell Parker was born in December of 1878; [Note: the census listed only the month and year of birth] B. James E. Parker was born in August, 1884; C. Jacob B. Parker was born in October, 1886; D. Nancy Alice Parker was born in July, 1888; E. Carrie [or Cannie?] K. Parker was born in July, 1890; F. Napolian C. Parker was born in March

1892; G. Laura E. Parker was born in June 1894; H. Jeannette Parker was born in April 1896; I. Zachariah P. Parker was born in June, 1899.

[Note: According to Gladys Gibbs of Old Fort, the following were the children of Charles and Melissa Moses Parker: A. Isabelle Parker was born in December of 1878 and married William Ammons; B. George Parker (no further info.); C. Memor Parker was born May 26, 1882 and died December 26, 1893; D. James E. Parker was born in August of 1884; E. Jacob B. was born in October of 1886; F. Nancy Alice was born in July of 1888 and married Levi Haskett; G. Connie or Cannie K. Parker was born in July of 1890; H. Napoleon C. Parker was born in March of 1892; I. Laura E. Parker was born in June of 1894; J. Jenette Parker was born in April of 1896.]

D. Nancy Alice Parker was born in July, 1888. She married Levi Haskett. Children of Levi and Alice Parker Haskett: a. Ethel Haskett; b. Levi Haskett.

a. Ethel Haskett was born March 29, 1918. She married Charlie Moore. Children of Charlie and Ethel Haskett Moore: 1. J.P. Moore was born June 1, 1938; 2. Maxine Moore was born November 18, 1939 and married Robert Dills; 3. Donnie Moore was born May 20, 1943; 4. Bobby J. Moore was born May 13, 1945; 5. Judy Moore was born December 8, 1946 and married Lester Stanfield; 6. Janice Moore was born June 24, 1950 and married David Baldwin.

III. The descendants of Frankie's granddaughter, Netter Elizabeth Parker. [Note: the name is listed as Phinetter in the 1860 census and Rhetor in an old family record.]

Netter Elizabeth Parker married a Barrett from Georgia. Their children: A. Bertha Barrett; B. Charles Barrett; C. Arby Barrett; and others not known.

A. Bertha Barrett had a son named Grover Barrett.

a. Grover Barrett married Bertha Sorrells. Children of Grover and Bertha Sorrells Barrett: 1. Branson Barrett married Evalee VanHook; 2. Conrad Barrett; 3. George Barrett married France Tallent; 4. Grace Barrett died young; 5. Dorothy Barrett; 6. Barbara Barrett married Ronald Gregory; 7. Willard Barrett married —— Hollbrook; 8. Harold Barrett.

1. Branson Barrett married Evalee Van Hook. Children of Branson and Evalee Van Hook Barrett: A. Jonetta Barrett married Larry Cloer; B. Elaine Barrett married Landy Holland and they were the parents of Landon Holland.

IV. The descendants of Frankie's granddaughter, Margaret Alice Parker:

Margaret Alice Parker was born February 1, 1859 and died at Gouges Creek in Mitchell County July 13, 1957. She married John Henry Makamey (called Mack) Thomas. Some of her descendants say that she was estranged from her mother because she felt the mother could have done more to hold the family together after their father was killed. Mack Thomas was born April 2, 1862 on Rose's Branch in Yancey County and died May 18, 1944 at Gouges Creek in Mitchell County. According to family tradition, the Thomases were of Spanish descent with short stocky builds and coal black hair. They are believed to have come from Florida to settle first along the French Broad River in what is now Buncombe and Madison counties in the late 1700s. Mack Thomas was the son of "Water Aaron" Thomas and Martha Jane Ollis. The older Thomases are buried at the Double Island Cemetery at Micaville in Yancey County, however, Mack and Alice Thomas and many of their descendants are buried at the old family cemetery on Gouges Creek in Mitchell County, which became the Gouge's Creek Baptist Church cemetery. The Thomas Family history was originally put together by Monroe Thomas and has been updated by his brother, Walter Thomas, and various other members of the family. The Thomas Family History was sent to me by Peggy Thomas Young of Johnson City, Tennesseee. I am grateful to Peggy Young for providing much of the more recent information on her family. Larry Biddix provided the dates from the family Bible of Mack and Alice Thomas, along with more recent information on his own family. Spruce Pine attorney Lloyd Hise Jr. provided the information on his branch of the family. Robert Buchanan of Asheville supplied the information on his branch.

Children of Mack and Alice Parker Thomas: 1. Wilburn Thomas; 2. Garrett Nellis "Poppy" Thomas; 3. Columbus Thomas; 4. Mitty Thomas; 5. Betty Thomas; 6. Minnie Thomas.

1. Wilburn Thomas was born July 18, 1883 in Mitchell County and died there November 6, 1962. A farmer and miner, he married Charlotte Burleson on September 24, 1905. She was born December 11, 1888 in Mitchell County, the daughter of Sam and Mary P. Burleson, and she died May 26, 1984. Children of Wilburn and Charlotte Burleson Thomas: A. Ruben Thomas; B. Mary Thomas; C. Dorothy Thomas; D. Clarence Thomas; E. Pansy Thomas; F. Baxter Ulyess Thomas; G. Fonzer Thomas; H. Julia Thomas; I. Monroe Lewis Thomas; J. Georgia Thomas.

A. Ruben Thomas was born October 28, 1905 and died July 4, 1945. He married Anna Duncan on March 1, 1930. Ruben died of drowning due to a boating accident in Lake James. He is buried in the Bear Creek Church cemetery in Mitchell County. Children of Ruben and Anna Duncan Thomas: a. Phillip Thomas; b. Mary Beth Thomas.

a. Philip Thomas was born November 5, 1931. He married Nancy E. Dale on June 23, 1957. Children of Philip and Nancy Dale Thomas: 1. Phyliss Anita Thomas was born October 2, 1959; 2. Douglas Keith Thomas was born October 1, 1964.

b. Mary Beth Thomas was born October 30, 1936. She married Bobby Lee Revis January 21, 1956. He died April 30, 1994 and is buried at Piney Branch Church Cemetery in Spruce Pine. Children of Bobby and Mary Beth Thomas Revis: 1. Allan Revis was born January 3, 1958; 2. Gregory Dwight Revis was born July 9, 1961 and married Maggie Church, May 6, 1988.

B. Mary Thomas was born April 26, 1907. She was first married to William Carpenter and second to Ben Biggerstaff, who was born November 14, 1888 and died in 1938. Both are buried in the Mt. Carmel Cemetery. Children of   William and Mary Thomas Carpenter: a. Betty Carpenter; b. Edith Carpenter; c. Frank Carpenter; d. William Carpenter Jr. Children of Ben and Mary Biggerstaff: f. Ray Biggerstaff; g. Bulah Ann Biggerstaff; h. Benny Biggerstaff was born December 11, 1944; i. Jimmy Biggerstaff married Myra Lynn Thomas, daughter of Frank and Alma Buchanan Thomas. Jimmy died of cancer on August 8, 1992.

f. Ray Biggerstaff was born in May of 1940 and shot and killed himself in November of 1984. He married Kay Sparks and they had one child: 1.Lisa Sparks who married Rodney Deyton and moved to Johnson City, Tennessee.

h. Benny Biggerstaff was born December 11, 1944. By his first marriage, he had one daughter, Michelle. He married a second time to Debbie Yelton. She was born February 25, 1956. Benny Biggerstaff shot and killed his wife and then himself on January 10, 1991. Their three children were raised by her mother and step-father, Everett and Jo Yelton Underwood. Children of Benny and Debbie Yelton Biggerstaff: 1. Leann Biggerstaff; 2. Kyle Biggerstaff; 3. Ryan Biggerstaff.

i. James David (Jimmy) Biggerstaff married Deborah Kerr. He died August 8, 1992. They had one child: 1. Chad Biggerstaff.

C. Dorothy Thomas was born March 25, 1909. She married Ernest

William Crowder, who died April 21, 1977. Children of Ernest and Dorothy Thomas Crowder: a. Lessie Crowder was born November 29, 1926; b. Lewis Crowder was born March 6, 1929; c. Lance Crowder was born April 25, 1931; d. Leonard Crowder was born April 21, 1934; e. Lillian Crowder was born June 4, 1937; f. Lela Crowder was born May 1, 1942; g. Lona Crowder was born May 1, 1944; h. Lydia Crowder was born March 25, 1946; i. Lanny Crowder was born July 24, 1955.

a. Lessie Crowder was born November 29, 1926. She first married a McClellan, second to —— Eaton and third to —— Eaton. Children of —— and Lessie Crowder McClellan: 1. Margret McClellan married —— Aberson and they were the parents of Dawn Aberson; 2. Stokes Ernest McClellan.

b. Lance Crowder was born April 25, 1931. Children: 1. Linda Crowder; 2. Susan Crowder.

c. Leonard Crowder was born April 21, 1934. He married Doris ——, who was born August 10, 1956. Children of Leonard and Doris Crowder: 1. Kathy Diane Crowder; 2. Mark Anthony Crowder.

1. Kathy Diane Crowder was born June 2, 1957. She married —— Hoover. Their children: A. Nathan Hoover; B. Amber Hoover.

2. Mark Anthony Crowder was born June 15, 1961.

Father of Cody Crowder.

d. Lillian Crowder was born June 4, 1937 and died November 1, 1993. Children: 1. J. Michael Still; 2. Donna Still.

e. Lela Crowder was born May 1, 1942. She married —— Singleton. Children: 1. Jeffrey Singleton; 2. Debbie Singleton; 3. Tiffany Singleton.

f. Lona Crowder was born May 1, 1944. She married —— Cable. Children: 1. Carolyn Cable; 2. Davida Cable; 3. Loretta Cable Cox; 4. Mary Cable; 5. Dennis Cable.

g. Lydia Crowder was born March 25, 1946. She married —— Banks. Children: 1. Sherry Banks Carson; 2. Nancy Banks McKinney; 3. Tina Banks; 4. Lisa Banks; 5. Stacy Banks.

D. Clarence Thomas was born December 21, 1911. He married May McClellan on September 16, 1933. She was born December 21, 1913. Children of Clarence and May McClellan Thomas: a. Jean Nancy Thomas was born February 24, 1934; b. Mary Alice Thomas was born January 2, 1937.

a. Jean Nancy Thomas was born February 24, 1934. She married William LeRoy McGuire, who was born December 9, 1933. He was a son of Howard and Effie Silvers McGuire. He died October 31, 1994. One child: 1.

Deborah Lee McGuire was born March 14, 1954. She married —— King on November 14, 1994 and lived in Blue Ridge, Ga. Three children.

E. Pansy Thomas was born June 25, 1913. She married Lloyd Hise, who was born January 6, 1914 and died July 14, 1977. He is buried in the Mt. Carmel Cemetery, Mitchell County. Children of Lloyd and Pansy Thomas Hise: a. Bobbie Jean Hise was born 1930 and died in 1997; b. Jessie Hise; c. Rosa Belle Hise; d. Ralph Hise; e. Lloyd Hise, Jr.; f. Phillip Hise.

a. Bobbie Jean Hise was born October 2, 1934 and died in 1997. She maried Jack English in 1953 and they had eight children: 1. Jerry Dean English; 2. Milton Steve English; 3. Lois English Greenlee; 4. eanette English Hoyle; 5. James Lloyd English; 6. Jimmy English; 7. Deborah English; 8. Mary Lou English.

b. Jessie William Hise was born June 19, 1936 and never married.

c. Rosa Belle Hise was born December 21, 1938 and married David Horton and they had two sons: 1. David Horton; 2. Victor Horton.

d. Ralph Edward Hise was born March 25, 1940 and was married twice. Children: 1. Amanda Hise; 2. Regina Hise; 3. Ralph Hise Jr.

e. Lloyd Hise Jr., an attorney in Spruce Pine since 1969, was born December 13, 1944. He was married and divorced. He is the father of one daughter: 1. Mary Beth Hise, a student at Warren Wilson College.

f. Phillip Wayne Hise was born August 15, 1946. He married Leisa Ellis and they had two daughters: 1. Allison Hise; 2. Adriane Hise. Philip Hise was a member of the Town Council in Spruce Pine.

F. Baxter Ulyess Thomas was born October 11, 1916. He married Connie Louise Freeman on March 7, 1935. The daughter of William Larkin and Fannie Elizabeth Blalock Freeman, she was born January 26, 1918. Baxter Thomas was killed on April 15, 1960 in his pickup truck on the Morganton highway. Children of Baxter and Connie Freeman Thomas: a. Polly Elizabeth Thomas; b. William Baxter Thomas; c. Peggy Lynn Thomas; d. Elsia Ruth Thomas.

a. Polly Elizabeth Thomas was born June 17, 1936. She married Wilt Bean on December 24, 1952. She married second to Ted Seward on May 5, 1977 in Oklahoma City, Okla. She married third to Blaney Qualls in Oklahoma City. She married fourth to C.B. Jones in Wister, Okla. Children of Wilt and Polly Thomas Beam: 1. Wanda Elizabeth Beam was born August 31, 1953; 2. Kim Louise Beam was born July 3, 1961.

b. William Baxter Thomas was born February 4, 1938. He married Rachel Jean Garland on July 4, 1964. She was born January 26, 1941. One child: 1.enny Jean Thomas was born March 20, 1965.

c. Peggy Lynn Thomas was born May 16, 1940. She married Ted Joe young, son of Merritt Crawford and Lillie Alberta Buchanan Young, on April 2, 1960. Ted and Peggy Young are the owners of Young's Printing and Bindery in Johnson City, Tenn. Ted served in the U.S. Navy from 1955-1959 on the USS New Jersey and the USS Shenandoah AD-26. Children of Ted and Peggy Thomas Young: 1. Timothy Lewis Young; 2. Delisa Lynn Young; 3. Tony Crawford Young.

1. Timothy Lewis Young was born August 30, 1961. He married Leslie Anne Greenwalt in Baltimore, Md., on June 29, 1985. She was born December 3, 1960 in Baltimore. Children: A. Emily Marie Young was born July 16, 1991; B. Sarah Elizabeth Young was born January 23, 1994; C. Samuel Thomas Young was born March 31, 1997.

2. DeLisa Lynn Young was born January 22, 1964. She married Charles Edward Wilkerson on September 2, 1989. Both worked as electrical engineers for NASA in Huntsville, Ala. Children: A. Brenna Lynn Wilkerson was born May 21, 1991; B. Charles Joseph Wilkerson was born May 24. 1994.

3. Tony Crawford Young was born September 24, 1969. He married Norma Jean "Sissie" Shepard, daughter of Rosco and Phyliss Shepard, on August 31, 1996.

d. Elsia Ruth Thomas was born June 26, 1942. She married Lee Ray Pitman on December 27, 1959. Children: 1. Donnie Ray Pitman; 2. Anita Lynn Pitman.

1. Donnie Ray Pitman was born May 13, 1960. He first married Connie Renee Hendrix on February 13, 1983. He married second in 1996 to Ruth Ann —. Children of Donnie and Connie Hendrix Pitman: A. Adam Pitman was born September 29, 1986 in Iredell County, N.C.; B. Austin Lee Pitman was born August 15, 1991 in DeKalb County, Ga.

2. Anita Lynn Pitman was born October 23, 1965. She married James Karl Jordan III. Children: A. James Karl Jordan IV was born July 20, 1990; B. Clint Ray Jordan was born June 17, 1993.

G. Fonzer Thomas was born May 8, 1918 and died September 1, 1994 at his home in Rutherfordton. He married Agnes McLellan in Spruce Pine on September 21, 1935. Children of Fonzer and Agnes McLellan Thomas: a. Billy Thomas; b. Betty Jean Thomas; c. Rosanna Thomas; d. Joseph Dale Thomas; e. Alan Keith Thomas.

H. Julia Thomas was born March 22, 1920. She married Paul McClellan, who was born April 24, 1915. Children of Paul and Julia Thomas McClellan: a. Betty Lou McClellan; b. Shirley Mae McClellan; c. Shelby Jean McClellan; d. Daniel Ray McClellan; e. Pauline Marie McClellan; f. Paul McClellan; g. Douglas McClellan; h. Ricky McClellan.

a. Betty Lou McClellan was born March 2, 1938. She married Thomas Earl Kesterson, who was born February 22, 1937. Children: 1. Terry Lee Kesterson was born February 8, 1957; 2. Billy Joe Kesterson was born July 16, 1959; 3. Thomas Earl Kesterson was born May 3, 1964.

b. Shirley Mae McClellan was born July 23, 1940. She married Richard Fisher in November 1966. He was born June 22, 1933 and died August 1982. One child: Michael R. Fisher was born September 3, 1957. He married Dorothy Lynn Morrisey in Cherokee County on December 13, 1987. She was born March 22, 1958.

c. Shelby Jean McClellan was born November 11, 1942. She was first married to Sherman Lee Swafford and second to Noah Canipe. Children of Sherman and Shelby McClellan Swafford:1. Sandy Scott Swafford; 2. Gary Lee Swafford.

1.Sandy Scott Swafford was born in April of 1960. He married Roxanne Sane and they had one child: William Tyler Swafford was born February 11, 1988.

2. Gary Lee Swafford was born July 1, 1962.

d. Daniel Ray McClellan was born January 31, 1946. He married Nancy J. Johnson on May 15, 1955. She was born May 18, 1946. Children: 1. Sheila McClellan; 2. Charlote McClellan; 3. Danielle McClellan.

1. Sheila McClellan was born September 22, 1966. She married —— Helms. Children: A. Sam Helms; B. Stephanie Helms.

e. Pauline Marie McClellan was born in 1944. On August 8, 1959, she married Aubrey A. Ferree, who was born April 15, 1935. Children: 1. Alton Scott Ferree; 2. Edward Lee Ferree.

1. Alton Scott Ferree was born May 24, 1966 in Rutherford County. He married Crystal Vance, who was born March 28, 1967. Children: A. Anthony Ray Ferree was born in January of 1985; B. Alton Scott Ferree Jr. was born in June, 1986; C. Andrew Lee Ferree was born in July 1988; D. Leigh Ann Ferree was born in November of 1990.

2. Edward Lee Ferree was born September 1, 1969.

f. Paul McClellan was born January 21, 1950. He married Karen ——. Children: 1. Rebecca McClellan; 2. Kelly McClellan; 3. Wendy McClellan.

g. Douglas McClellan

h. Ricky McClellan

I. Monroe Lewis Thomas was born February 19, 1923. He married Maude Etta Trivett, who was born January 18, 1924. Children: a. Kenneth Lewis Thomas; b. Phillip Wayne Thomas; c. James (Tommy) Moses Thomas; d. Bonnie Lou Thomas; e. Samuel Dean Thomas; f. Donnie Richard Thomas; g. Shirley Dianne Thomas;. Dennie Jack Thomas; i. Janice Lynn Thomas.

a. Kenneth Lewis Thomas was born February 10, 1945. On July 2, 1966, he married Mary Jo Lipps, who was born May 30, 1944. One child: Melissa Thomas was born September 24, 1971.

b. Phillip Wayne Thomas was born June 2, 1946. He served from 1966 to 1968 in the Vietnam War. He married Stella Fisher, who was born June 26, 1950. Children: 1. Stacy Wayne Thomas; 2. Shane Eric Thomas.

1. Stacy Wayne Thomas was born February 28, 1970. He married Amy Mathis. Children: A. Ashley Danielle Thomas; B. Drianna Elizabeth Thomas.

2. Shane Eric Thomas was born September 10, 1972. He married in Norfolk, Va., on August 26, 1995 to Dawn Heather Nussbaum, daughter of Mike and Diane Nussbaum.

c. James (Tommy) Moses Thomas was born June 11, 1947. On June 7, 1969, he married Mary L. McKinney, who was born October 19, 1946. Children: 1. Meritta Kay Thomas; 2. Carmella Louise Thomas.

1. Meritta Kay Thomas was born September 5, 1991.

2. Carmella Louise Thomas was born July 15, 1977.

d. Bonnie Lou Thomas was born October 27, 1948. She married first to Lewis E. Honeycutt and second, on August 29, 1982, to Oscar T. Benfield, who was born September 12, 1940. Children: 1. Lisa Lynn Honeycutt was born January 12, 1969 and died August 4, 1972; 2. Teresa Gayle Benfield was born February 6, 1972.

e. Samuel Dean Thomas was born June 4, 1950

f. Donnie Richard Thomas was born March 8, 1952. On April 13, 1975, he married Susan Elaine Forbes, who was born June 11, 1957. Children: 1. Holly Lane Thomas was born June 4, 1978; 2. Alisha Lindsy Thomas was born September 11, 1982; 3. Jody Don Thomas was born December 21, 1987.

g. Shirley Dianne Thomas was born December 31, 1953

h. Dennie Jack Thomas was born July 27, 1955. He married Pamela Jane Ollis, who was born June 1, 1959. She was a daughter of Frank "Pete" and

Evelyn Thomas Ollis.

i. Janice lynn Thomas was born May 19, 1959 and died of cancer on April 19, 1970.

J. Georgia Thomas married Guy McClellan. Children: a. Joyce McClellan; b. Wanda McClellan; c. Mary McClellan; d. Sally McClellan.

a. Joyce McClellan was married on November 28, 1964 to Richard Wayne Burleson, who was born April 25, 1946. Children: 1. Tammie Marie Burleson was born October 11, 1968; 2. Guy Wayne Burleson was born December 21, 1973.

b. Wanda McClellan was born June 25, 1950. On March 29, 1969, she married Billy Ray Hoilman, who was born October 30, 1948. One child: 1. Darren Alfred Hoilman was born January 28, 1973.

c. Mary McClellan was born April 5, 1953. On November 26, 1971, she married Bobby Carpenter, who was born November 28, 1949. One child: 1. Michelle Lee Carpenter was born September 22, 1979.

2. Garrett Nellis "Poppy" Thomas was born August 13, 1885 and died December 12, 1975. He married Ida Duncan, daughter of John and Millie Pittman Duncan, who was born October 15, 1889 and died September 12, 1955. Children of Poppy and Ida Duncan Thomas: A. John Thomas; B. Scott W. Thomas; C. Chesley Chet Thomas; D. May Belle Thomas; E. Verda Lee Thomas.

A. John Thomas was born October 13, 1913 in Mitchell County and died August 13, 1975 in the VA hospital in Salisbury.

B. Scott W. Thomas was born September 12, 1915. On December 16, 1933, he married Osa McClellan, who was born in 1914. He died July 4, 1985 and is buried in Temple Mountain Baptist Church cemetery in Mitchell County. Children: a. Scott J. Thomas; b. Ola Belle Thomas; c. Jack Ray Thomas; d. Evelyn Thomas.

a. Scott J. Thomas was born November 18, 1934. On August 10, 1958 in Little Rock, Ark., he married Martha Jo Anderson, who was born November 1, 1938. A veteran of the U.S. Air Force, he died July 1, 1997. Children: 1. Dan Keith Thomas; 2. Audrey Jo Thomas.

1. Dan Keith Thomas was born June 9, 1959.

2. Audrey Jo Thomas was born October 27, 1962. She married David Thompson. Children: A. Thomas Allen Thompson; B. Sarah Beth Thompson; C. Steven Browning Thompson.

b. Ola Belle Thomas was born August 15, 1936. On December 29, 1954, she married Jimmy Donald Canipe, who was born January 12, 1934 in

Mecklenburg County and died at Charlotte May 25, 1991. Children: 1. Regina Gail Canipe was born December 13, 1957; 2. Jimmy Donald Canipe Jr. was born May 8, 1963.

c. Jack Ray Thomas was born July 12, 1938. On September 14, 1958, he married Glenda Fisher, who was born October 11, 1942. One child: Veneisa Lee Thomas was born February 16, 1961.

d. Evelyn Thomas was born July 11, 1941. On August 31, 1956, she married Frank "Pete" Ollis, who was born June 23, 1936. Children: 1. Angela Marie Ollis; 2. Pamela J. Ollis; 3. Larry Shane Ollis.

1. Angela Marie Ollis was born April 16, 1958. She married William Ray Justice. One child: Jason Scott Justice was born October 25, 1975.

2. Pamela Jane Ollis was born June 1, 1959. She married Dennis Jack Thomas, son of Monroe Lewis and Maude Trivett Thomas, and who was born July 29, 1955.

3. Larry Shane Ollis was born May 9, 1971. On October 24, 1992, he married Connie Alisa Cornett.

C. Chesley Chet Thomas was born October 10, 1909. He married Ola Greenen, who was born in 1909 and died in 1984. He died June 13, 1969. Children: a. Frank Thomas; b. Fay Thomas; c. Cosa Lee Thomas; R.C. Thomas

a. Frank Thomas was born February 7, 1929. He married on January 8, 1949 to Alma Buchanan, who was born August 25, 1929. He served in the Army for five years and the Air Force for two years. Their son, Frank Thomas Jr. died at three days old July 13, 1953 and they adopted two other children: 1. Myra Lynn Thomas; 2. Lisa Marie Thomas.

1. Myra Lynn Thomas

2. Lisa Marie Thomas.

D. May Belle Thomas was born January 22, 1907. She married Fonzer Buchanan, son of Mack and Peggy Ward Buchanan. He was born April, 1923. May Thomas Buchanan died August 21, 1996. Children:a. Taylor Buchanan; b. Jack Buchanan; c. Marjorie Buchanan; d. Charles Buchanan.

a. Taylor Buchanan was born December 1, 1924. Children: 1. Gwynne Lee Buchanan; 2. Wayne Thomas Buchanan 3. John Taylor Buchanan.

1. Gwynne Lee Buchanan was born January 21, 1949

2. Wayne Thomas Buchanan was born January 28, 1950 and died July 21, 1973.

3. John Taylor Buchanan was born April 15, 1973.

b. Jack Buchanan was born April 15, 1926.

c. Marjorie Buchanan was born June 30, 1927. On July 13, 1946, she married Emmet Gregory Cowan in Rossville, Ga. Children: 1. Laura Dianne Cowan; 2. Linda Lee Cowan.

1. Laura Dianne Cowan was born August 28, 1949. She first married Brinson Wesley Savage Jr. on July 8, 1968; she married second to Glyn Ralph Worrock on October 3, 1975 in Portsmouth, Va.; she married third to David Acron Cooper III, in Aiken, S.C., on April 30, 1988. Children: A. Andrea Tracey Savage was born October 14, 1971; B. Gregory Damon Worrock was born May 1, 1977.

d. Charles Buchanan was born November 24, 1930

E. Verda Lee Thomas was born September 5, 1911. She was first married to Fate Ward and second to William J. Lusk. She died January 29, 1994. Children of Fate and Verda Thomas Ward: a. Ralph Ray Ward; b. Ruth Lee Ward; c. Lee Roy Ward.

a. Ralph Ray Ward was born April 10, 1932. On July 18, 1959, he married Bulah Anne Freeman, who was born March 1, 1938, a daughter of Robert Adam and Artha Betty Woody Freeman. Children: 1. Ralph Ray Ward Jr. was born April 25, 1952 in Muskegee, Ga.; 2. Gary Lee Ward was born March 26, 1953 in Muskegee. Ralph served in the U.S. Army from 1949 to 1955 and was a Korean veteran.

3. David Columbus Thomas was born August 29, 1888. He first married Buna Wyatt, daughter of Jonas and Mary Polly Woody Wyatt. He married a second time to Lillie McClellan. Children of Columbus and BunaWyatt Thomas:

A. Fred Thomas married Velva Buchanan.

B. Ethel Thomas was born in 1905. She married Clarence Homer Buchanan, who was born in 1899. He was a son of Lafayette and Susan (Sudie) Freeman Buchanan. Children: a. Burt Buchanan; b. Geneva Buchanan; c. Velva Buchanan; d. Calvin Buchanan; e. Harold Buchanan; f. Robert Buchanan.

a. Burt Buchanan was born December 4, 1924 and died July 17, 1948.

b. Calvin Buchanan was born January 26, 1927. He married Edith Hall Moody.

c. Genevieve Buchanan was born July 9, 1929. She married Clifton Holder and they had one son, Roger Holder, who was born December 27, 1948.

d. Dorothy Buchanan was born February 23, 1931. She married James Trivett and they had three children:

1. Gerald Trivett was born May 24, 1953. He married Lynn Stroup.

2. Rachel Trivett was born January 12, 1956. She married Kenneth Murdock.

3. Charles Trivett was born April 28, 1958. He married Wanda Cook and they had one child: Christy Trivett.

f. Robert Buchanan was born September 27, 1940. He married Martha Horton on November 12, 1965. They had one son, Bruce Buchanan who was born November 12, 1970.

g. Velva L. Buchanan was born July 28, 1943. She married Joe Franklin and they had two children: A. Chris Franklin was born June 10, 1967; B. Brian Franklin was born March 8, 1974.

C. Mack Thomas married Ruth Harrison. Children of Mack and Ruth Harrison Thomas:

a. Mary Jo Thomas

b. George Thomas

D. Harold Thomas was born March 3, 1913 and died in 1973. He married Ethel Duncan. Children of Harold and Ethel Duncan Thomas:

a. Gail Thomas Bunn. Children: 1. Leslie Bunn; 2. Steven Bunn.

b. Nelle Thomas Glenn. One child: 1. James Glenn.

c. Margaret Thomas McGraw. Children: 1. Thomas McGraw; 2. John McGraw.

d. Freddy Thomas Jones.

E. Maud Thomas was born March 19, 1916 and died January 27, 1917.

4. Bettie Jane Thomas was born November 3, 1890. She married Cleve Silvers. Children of Cleve and Betty Thomas Silvers:

A. Effie Silvers was born about 1916 and died January 4, 1996 in New Jersey. She is buried in Mt. Carmel Church Cemetery in Mitchell County. She married Howard McGuire. Children: a. William LeRoy McGuire; b. Hazel McGuire; c. Linda McGuire; d. George Ray McGuire.

a. William LeRoy McGuire was born December 9, 1933. He married Jean Thomas.

b. Hazel Mcguire married ――Forbes and moved to Edison, N.J.

c. Linda McGuire married ――Lowder

d. George Ray McGuire.

B. Lena Silvers married ――Beam and they had two sons: 1. Ralph Beam; 2. Parker Beam. Parker Beam married Wilma ――and they had two sons. He died in 1995. Ralph Beam married Buna Presnell.

C. Woodrow Silvers died at age 13 in a hunting accident.

5. Mittie Loretta Thomas was born April 30, 1894. She married Timothy Johnson Pitman, son of Wilburn and Mary Silver Pitman. Mary Silver Pitman was the daughter of Reuben and Sarah Ann Sparks Silver. Reuben was the son of Jacob Silver and his second wife and was a half-brother to Charles Silver. Children: A. Kennith Theo Pitman; B. Wilbur Ernest Pitman; C. Avery Franklin Pitman; D. Edith Eleonor Pitman;E. Arnold Lee Pitman.

A. Kennith Theo Pitman was born June 5, 1913. He was married twice, first to Ada Gunter. Kennith and Ada Gunter Pitman had one child, Carl Pitman.

a. Carl Pitman married Frances Gravotte and they had two children: Curtis Pitman and Vicky Pitman.

Kennith Pitman moved to Mobile, Alabama, as a young man and changed his name to Keely Theodore Parker, taking the surname of his grandmother, Margaret Alice Parker. Kelly Parker married a second time to Dorris Dueitt of Mississippi and they had four children:

b. Carol Parker was born November 9, 1947.

c. Kelly T. Parker was born February 21, 1953.

d. Mildred Parker was born November 6, 1950.

e. Timothy Parker was born January 29, 1956.

B. Wilbur Ernest Pitman was born May 9, 1917 and died June 17, 1917.

C. Avery Franklin Pitman was born May 3, 1920. A member of the 82nd Airborne Division, he died at Normandy, France, June 15, 1944 and is buried in the American cemetery there.

D. Edith Eleonor Pitman was born August 9, 1925 and died November 7, 1966. She married Harold G. Biddix, son of Robert B. and Effy Snyder Biddix. Children of Harold and Edith Pitman Biddix: a. Alma Kay Biddix; b. Larry A. Biddix.

a. Alma Kay Biddix was born September 29, 1944 and died September 22, 1982. She married Paul Mack Ramsey Jr.

b. Larry A. Biddix was born November 26, 1946. He married Brenda L. Calloway, daughter of Stokes and Trula Hughes Calloway. Children of Larry and Brenda Calloway Biddix: 1. Alan Lee Biddix; 2. Eva Denay Biddix; 3. Holly Jeanette Biddix.

1. Alan Lee Biddix was born August 11, 1971.He married Casandra Blazer. Children: A. Devon Lee Ann Biddix was born August 29, 1992; B. Jacob Cain Biddix was born August 31, 1993.

2. Eva Denay Biddix was born October 10, 1974 and is the mother of one

child: Edith Allison, who was born December 22, 1991.

3. Holly Jeanette Biddix was born February 14, 1976. She married Michael Oltrogge.

E. Arnold Lee Pitman was born April 27, 1930 and died after only a few hours the same day.

6. Minnie Thomas was born May 22, 1897 and died October 29, 1963. She married Dexter "Deck" Arthur Buchanan, who was born July 20, 1891 and died July 29, 1979. Children of Deck and Minnie Thomas Buchanan:

A. Alice Buchanan.

B. Brown Buchanan married Mary Buchanan.

C. Lonnie C. Buchanan was born in 1925 and died June 12, 1994. He married Evelyn Ledford. Children: a. Patricia Buchanan Fisher; b. Rita Buchanan; c. Darrell Buchanan; d. Jim Buchanan.

D. Texie Buchanan was born December 16, 1918. She married Ernest Jones.

E. Tessie Buchanan married John McLellan.

F. Howard Buchanan married Betty Johnson. Children: a. Renee Buchanan; b. Karen Buchanan; c. Lavada Buchanan.

G. Virgie Buchanan.

H. Ivy Buchanan married Oscar McClellan.

V. The descendants of Frankie's granddaughter, Magdalina Mariah Parker:

Mary Ann or Myra or Magdalina Mariah Parker was born March 1, 1861 and died November 11, 1949. She married William T. Gregory, son of Henry Jackson and Mary C. "Polly" Blackburn Gregory. He was born March 18, 1855 and died September 22, 1937. Children of William and Mariah Parker Gregory: A. Benjamin Harrison Gregory; B. Laura C. Peggy Gregory; C. Parker Gregory; D. Minnie Gregory; E. Sallie Gregory; F. Alice Gregory, G. Alex Gregory; H. Theodore Gregory.

A. Benjamin Harrison Gregory, born in February of 1891, married Mary Melinda Taylor. Children of Benjamin and Mary Taylor Gregory: a. Pearl Gregory; b. Edgar Gregory; c. Lois Gregory; d. Lester Gregory; e. Lester Gregory; f. Lewis Gregory.

B. Laura C. "Peggy" Gregory, born in October of 1893, married James Ammons. Children of James and Laura Gregory Ammons: a. Minnie Ammons; b. Lela Ammons; c. ora Ammons; d. Harrison Ammons; e Fred Ammons; f. Parker Ammons; g.Myrtle Ammons.

C. John W. Gregory was born May 11, 1894 and died July 15, 1930. He married Lee Collins. hildren of John and Lee Collins Gregory: a. Ray Gregory; b. Roy Gregory; c. Lloyd Gregory; d. John Gregory; e.Edna Gregory.

D. Parker Gregory, born in March of 1896, married Lelia Woodard. Children of Parker and Lelia Woodard Gregory: a. Ruby Gregory Ammons; b. Dr. Keith Gregory; c. James B. Gregory; d. John Hayes Gregory; e. Charles B. Gregory; f. Wayne Edwin Gregory.

E. Minnie E. Gregory, born in March of 1897, married Dan Buchanan. Children of Dan and Minnie Gregory Buchanan: a. Hilda Buchanan; b. Claude Buchanan; c. Earl Buchanan; d. Rose Buchanan; e. Lola Buchanan; f. Nick Buchanan; g. Eloise Buchanan; h. Floyd (Smoky) Buchanan.

F. Sallie Gregory, born in March of 1898, married William "Will" M. Buchanan. Children of Will and Sallie Gregory Buchanan: a. Mary Buchanan; b. Mattie Buchanan; c.Maude Buchanan; d. Fred Buchanan; e. Lelia Buchanan; f. Lydia Buchanan; g. Dee Buchanan; h. Allie Buchanan; i. Vera Buchanan; j. Theodore Buchanan; k. Lucille Buchanan.

G. Jim Gregory married Myrtle Breedlove.

H. Alex Gregory married Oletia Corbin.

I. Alice Gregory married Robert Fox. Children of Robert and Alice Gregory Fox: a.ady Fox; b.ssie Fox; c. Wade Fox; d. Hazel Fox.

J. Theodore Gregory was born August 5, 1906 and died June 24, 1941.

VI. The descendants of Frankie's granddaughter, Cansada, or Kasada, or Kansas Parker:

Cansada, or Kasada, or Kansas Parker was born in 1860 and died December 13, 1894. She married Jesse G. Owens. [No further information.]

Bibliography

Note: All primary, or original, sources will be found in Part IV of this book. This bibliography refers only to books and articles written about Frankie Silver.

Arthur, John Preston, *History of Western North Carolina*, Raleigh, N.C., Edwards & Broughton, 1917. His account is similar to that published in *Cabins in the Laurel* and comes from the same interview with Lucinda Norman, half sister of Charles Silver.

Avery, Clifton K., editor, *Official Court Record of the Trial, Conviction and Execution of Francis Silvers, First Woman Hanged in North Carolina.* From the minutes of the Burke County Superior Court, Morganton, North Carolina: The *News-Herald*, 1953.

Battle, Kemp Plummer, *Memories of an Old-Time Tar Heel*, Chapel Hill, University of North Carolina Press, 1945.

Burt, Olive Woolley, editor, *American Murder Ballads and Their Stories*, New York, Oxford University Press, 1958. 272 pages.

Bryant, "Red Buck" H.E.C., "The Horrible Deed of a Wife," *Charlotte Daily Observer*, March 22, 1903; page 10. This article was widely reprinted in numerous newspapers over the years and in two books: in Robert B. Phillips' *One of God's Children in Toe River Valley*, pages 95-102, and also in James Turpin's weird little book called *The Serpent Slips into a Modern Eden*, published in Raleigh in 1923 and focused on a more recent case.

Ervin, Eunice, "Forgotten Village," Morganton, (1816-1865,) 1935.

Ervin, Samuel J. Jr., "Frankie Silver," article in the *Morganton News-Herald*, April 3, 1924.

Ervin, Samuel J. Jr., *Burke County Courthouses and Related Matters, Morganton*, Morganton, Historic Burke Foundation, 1985, page 27.

Morganton News-Herald, other articles on Frankie Silver: "Recalls Ghost of Two in Old Tragedy," February 5, 1931; "Legends Have Grown Up About Frankie Silvers," March 27, 1964.

Hiergesell, Geneva. Feature articles in the *Morganton News-Herald*: "When They Hanged Frankie Silvers in Burke," January 29, 1968l; "Here's More About Poor Frankie Silvers," February 13, 1968; "Burke Man Has an Old Article About Frankie Silvers," March 28, 1968.

Joslin, Michael, "Frankie and Charley: A new look at an old crime," *Mitchell News-Journal*, October 1, 1997. Joslin identifies Frankie as "the first white woman in the state to suffer that fate [hanging]."

Laws, Malcolm, *Native American Balladry: A Descriptive Study and a Bibliographical Syllabus*, Philadelphia, American Folklore Society, 1964, page 268.

McCall, Maxine, *They Won't Hang a Woman*, Burke County Public Schools, 1972.

Menzies, Robert and Smith, Edmond, "The Scarlet Enigma of Toe River," *True Detective Mysteries* magazine, July 1935.

Menzies, Robert, "Charlie Silver was playing loose with the Gals but Frankie Brought him low," *The News and Observer*, October 10, 1937.

Nash, L.A., "Only Woman Ever Hanged in State Lived in Burke," *Greensboro Daily News*, November 5, 1939.

Parris, John, in *The Asheville Citizen*, "Frankie Silvers' Poem," September 29, 1955, and "Ellis Cove Killer First Woman Hanged in North Carolina," July 22, 1988 The first column was also reprinted in *Roaming the Mountains with John Parris*, Edwards & Broughton Co., Raleigh, 1955.

Phifer, Edward W. Jr., Burke: *The History of a North Carolina County, 1777-1920*, Morganton, Phifer, 1982, page 344.

Sakowski, Carolyn, "The Life and Death of Frankie Silvers," master's thesis, Appalachian State University May, 1972.

Sheppard, Muriel Earley, *Cabins in the Laurel*, Chapel Hill, University of North Carolina Press, 1935.

Wellman, Manly Wade, *Dead and Gone: Classic Crimes of North Carolina*, Chapel Hill, N.C., UNC Press, 1954.

Wellman, Manly Wade, "Song from the Scaffold," *The News and Observer*, February 1, 1953.

Wise, Jim, "What Frankie Did," *Durham Morning Herald*, September 14, 1997. Wise wrote of Frankie Silver: "In 1833, she became the only white woman ever hanged by the State of North Carolina."

Yancey, Noel, "Murderer's Poetic Plea," *Spectator*, (Raleigh, N.C.),. October 18, 1984.

Young, Perry Deane, "Frankie Silver and the Laws of God and Man," in *Heritage of the Toe River Valley*, edited by Lloyd Bailey, 1994.

Young, Perry Deane, "Why Frankie Silver Swung," *Ms.* magazine, May 1976.

Young, Perry Deane, "In the Mountains, There's a Tale of Christmas," *Durham Morning Herald*, December 22, 1962. I do not recommend this one.